THE GOLDEN BLADE

LIGHT ON LIFE

2000

52nd EDITION

Anthroposophy springs from the work and teaching of Rudolf Steiner. He described it as a path of knowledge, to guide the spiritual in the human being to the spiritual in the universe.

The aim of this annual journal is to bring the outlook of anthroposophy to bear on questions and activities relevant to the present, in a way which may have lasting value. It was founded in 1949 by Charles Davy and Arnold Freeman, who were its first editors.

The title derives from an old Persian legend, according to which King Jamshid received from his god, Ahura Mazda, a golden blade with which to fulfil his mission on earth. It carried the heavenly forces of light into the darkness of earthly substance, thus allowing its transformation. The legend points to the possibility that humanity, through wise and compassionate work with the earth, can one day regain on a new level what was lost when the Age of Gold was supplanted by those of Silver, Bronze and Iron. Technology could serve this aim; instead of endangering our planet's life, it could help to make the earth a new sun.

LIGHT ON LIFE

Edited by William Forward, Simon Blaxland-de Lange
and Andrew Wolpert

The Golden Blade

First published in 1999 by The Golden Blade

The Editors
The Golden Blade
Emerson College
Forest Row
East Sussex RH18 5JX
England

ISBN 0-9531600-2-5
ISSN 0967-6708

Printed in Great Britain
by Design To Print, Forest Row, East Sussex

Contents

Editorial Notes

The last three issues of this journal have focussed, in one way or another, on the theme of our destiny as human beings poised between the spiritual world of our origin and the earthly world in which, for a brief span, we endeavour to find our place, form relationships with others and contribute towards the unfolding destiny of mankind and the Earth as a whole. This choice of theme has been guided by the conviction that, as human individuals gifted with the capacity of independent thinking and judgement, men and women of today already hold in their hands the key to transforming their lives in accordance with their deepest ideals. There is a widespread assumption that, despite all the colossal evidence to the contrary from man's creativity over the ages, human intelligence is wholly the product of material forces, and, hence, has neither cognitive nor moral authority over the material world; but this does not mean that it is in any sense invalid to mark the passage from one century, and one millennium, to another by continuing in this present issue to dwell upon the true source of what we see around us, namely, man himself.

But there is another, more tangible, justification for distancing oneself from the millennial celebration of the triumphs of materialism, with its twin poles of euphoria and the extreme anguish which recognition of the effects of these triumphs generates. (Incidentally, it is perhaps not for nothing that the new millennium is generally being celebrated at the beginning of the year nought, i.e. in the last year of the second millennium). For, contrary to what is often supposed by those who, understandably enough perhaps, experience the world as being increasingly dominated by economic forces that demean the human spirit and political forces that enslave the human soul, there has over recent years been a steady growth in a consciousness of a different kind. This is exemplified in the "civic" consciousness referred to in an article by Nicanor Perlas in the July 1999 issue of *Anthroposophy Worldwide,* a consciousness which takes as its focus local, land-based, people-centred initiatives and is also associated with what Perlas refers to as "cultural creatives", a term which denotes "the people behind global civil society, responsible governance and socially responsible business". Perlas goes on to clarify what he considers to be the values held by cultural creatives: "nature as sacred, search for communities, limits to growth, meaningful relationships, spirituality, adverse to corporate polluters, altruism, meditative path, holistic health, green values, earth as a living organism, globalism, love for the foreign and so on". As a tiny example of the way in which the human element is now able to stand up for itself in the popular mind against the apparent tidal wave of "progress", there was a report in the *Guardian* dated 26th July of Norfolk Council's attempt to introduce a <u>voluntary</u> policy giving pedestrians, cyclists and farm traffic priority on country roads. The newspaper - or at any rate the article's headline - described this as an attempt to turn the clock back, which of course altogether misses the point.

What is, however, of particular interest for our present purposes is that this same "cultural creative" attitude can be discerned in a series of widely acclaimed biographies of notable figures in the Romantic Movement which have been published in recent years; and it is this penetration of what can only be described as a spiritual-scientific discipline into the forefront of the modern academic world which has been the inspiration for the present issue of this journal. Thus both Dorit Winter and Coralee Schmandt focus explicitly on this phenomenon, with Dorit writing in the first instance out of her reaction to an event of some notoriety in American politics which was omnipresent at the time but has scarcely become any less relevant now, and Coralee approaching the same phenomenon more from the side of the life of Coleridge in particular. Henning Köhler and Mathias Wais each offer contributions which describe in their different ways some of the fruits of their work in discerning meaningful patterns in what might otherwise be seen as a haphazard series of biographical events; and they draw attention to the practical value and the therapeutic benefit of research of this kind. Doré Deverell and Nick Thomas give direct, spontaneous accounts of certain crucial events in their lives which have led to their present life-involvements. Bob Dudney's article offers a medical perspective to this theme of living out a human life in our time. The series of articles is concluded by a second contribution written out of a medical perspective. In the 1998 edition of the *Golden Blade* entitled "Working with Destiny" we published an article by Jostein Saether under the heading "Research Techniques and Life Events". Subsequently Saether has written other articles about his work and given lectures, some of which have found a critical audience. We have included in this issue part of an article by three Norwegian anthroposophical doctors published in the Norwegian anthroposophical newsletter, giving their reasons for questioning Saether's methods and results. The *Golden Blade* for the year 2000 concludes with a review of a book which reflects upon the phenomena of evil confronting 20th and 21st century humanity as, on the one hand, a source of impediment to its path into the future and, on the other, a challenge to develop precisely those qualities addressed by the preceding articles.

We are very grateful to Anne Stockton for the cover illustration, which so artistically reproduces an extraordinary cosmic-geological phenomenon. In the remoteness of the Chaco Canyon in the desert of New Mexico, near the Kiva Circles and the ruined foundations of the city of the Anasazi Indians, three parallel flat rocks rise up and lean against the great Butte mass, and there on the shadowed rock nineteen concentric rings were incised over a thousand years ago. At the solstices and the equinoxes a spot of light appears at the top of the outside ring, and like liquid gold flows down ring-edge by ring-edge forming this dagger of light. The artist Anna Soafer, backpacking on a remote outward-bound trail, noticed the carving on the rock and, returning many times, eventually discovered the connection with the sun. The film she made inspired Anne Stockton who, struck by its connection with the name and intentions of this journal, has recreated that event for the cover of this issue.

For the next (2001) issue of the *Golden Blade* we shall be inviting contributions from a younger generation of writers and readers, from those who are carrying the new spiritual impulses which will bear fruit in the millennium whose actual beginning that year will mark.

Glimmers of Truth

Dorit Winter

Not since Pinocchio has so much attention been given to whether an individual was telling the truth. Unlike Mr Clinton, however, Pinocchio incurred immediate and absolute correction. Things are no longer quite that simple. We now live in a world which spurns the very notion of truth as such. As a recent Newsweek article put it: "Science is predicated on the notion that all 'Truths' are merely tentative, ready to be overturned by the next discovery.... Without the capacity to delete and erase, there would be no way to evolve government, culture or ethics."[1] The metaphor is technology and the mentality is revisionist. Hit the delete button and truth is reinvented, answerability for words and actions conveniently disposed.

The shenanigans in the White House put truth on the front page. But as Monica became the media frenzy subject of the year, and truth became the world's cover story, truth itself got lost. The more the media pursued the story, the more they confirmed the fragility of truth as a concept. Not only did the Starr investigation merely confirm what most people already knew, that yes and no are interchangeable, that guilty or not guilty are the consequence of legal arbitration and that truth and morality, as the polls proved, are unrelated, it also degraded the word *Truth*. The more truth and lies took center stage in the story, the more was the name of Truth taken in vain, and *Truth,* the way a spiritual scientist conceives of it, undone. And yet....

And yet, "Man must have the possibility to lie, in order to

discover truth independently. He must gain the truth as an independent being, this is why Ahriman is there..."[2]

Every September for the past 10 years I have found myself trying to guide students entering the San Francisco Waldorf Teacher Training into the extremely challenging proposition that there is such a thing as Truth, that there is such a thing a Beauty, and that there is such a thing as Goodness, and that these three things are not relative, nor are they a matter of personal opinion or personal need. They are as objective as phenomena of color or tone, and they are the basis of Waldorf education. Furthermore, that unless these concepts become a matter of knowledge, rather than of belief, Waldorf education will remain merely an abstraction, rather than the active science it in fact is, and that an important part of the three years of the training is finding a relationship to this knowledge.

It is perhaps the greatest barrier facing the incoming students. anthroposophy is not a religion, and yet anthroposophical truth is cosmic truth; anthroposophy <u>is</u> truth; spiritual science means spiritual truth. Rudolf Steiner's efforts to make this clear fill his works. To give a sense of the scope and context of those efforts, I will cite two examples. In a sequence of lectures from 1911, published as GA 127 with the title *The Mission of the New Spiritual Revelation* and not yet translated into English, the theme of Truth arises again and again. In a supplement at the end of that volume, in some notes made in preparation for the establishment of a new anthroposophical branch in Heidenheim, Rudolf Steiner formulates "three clarion calls." The first was the call humanity heard from Mt. Sinai, the Law of Jehova. The second was the call of John the Baptist. "The third call, my dear friends, is the one which will declare the new revelations from the spiritual world through spiritual science."[3] This is unequivocal. Anthroposophy reveals spiritual truth. Truth. In the volume entitled *Das Christliche Mysterium* (1906-1907, GA 97), parts of which were recently published as *The Christian Mystery*, the meaning is unmistakable: "Spiritual science should help people to understand what human beings have in common; it should bring a higher wisdom - the spirit of Truth."[4]

Ahriman's obfuscations intensify. But the truth that is spiritual science, the truth "that is so urgently needed to serve the human soul as living nourishment, like bread, like air,"[5] the truth that is being repressed with ever greater mastery, is also now percolating up in ever clearer utterances. In the world-at-large, insights which we know to be corroborated by anthroposophical spiritual science are finding their way to the surface of human consciousness. Glintings of truth-arrived-at-independently are surfacing from beneath the crushing sludge of truth-homogenized.

It is incumbent upon us, who stand on the firm foundations of our anthroposophic strivings, to recognise those who, without the benefit of the "living nourishment" of anthroposophy, are, nevertheless, wresting truth from the abyss. For theirs is an isolated consciousness, not sustained by the vast truths of spiritual science, and it warrants our support.

We anthroposophists scour the word for people who can support us. And surely we can use such support. But we ought also to be attentive to those whose voices we recognise, so that we might offer our humble appreciation, our grateful acknowledgement.

In what follows I would like to make such an attempt.

Imagination as a Path to Truth

Spiritual Science shows us that Imagination is the preliminary step toward Inspiration and then Intuition. Thus Imagination is a goal for every seeking anthroposophist.

In *The Christian Mysteries*, in the context of the Rosicrucian quest for truth, Rudolf Steiner relates the ordinary poetic imagination to the heightened capacity for true thinking that is Imagination. He says: "When we know how to seek it and are mature enough, the truth can be found everywhere." And, "One acquires imagination by seeing everything emblematically."[6]
Here we have the connection between the great poets and truth.

And sometimes, those who investigate the evolution of the poetic sensibility catch the glow of truth revealed, and reflect it as biography.

Two recent biographies of writers already "owned" by anthroposophy manage just such illumination. They reveal the American Transcendentalist, Ralph Waldo Emerson, and the English Romanticist, Samuel Taylor Coleridge.

In such books as *What Coleridge Thought* and *Romanticism Comes of Age*, Owen Barfield has brilliantly documented Coleridge's inherent connection to spiritual science. As for Emerson, the existence of Emerson College speaks worlds about that connection. Simply stated, both Emerson and Coleridge grasp the truth. Profoundly Goethean in their perceptions, they looked upon nature and man as a script to be deciphered and arrive at anthroposophically "proven" truths. Both of them were brilliantly learned. Each was able to synthesize a review of civilization's texts with a genius for imaginative seeing, and both kept track of their own evolving consciousness. It is tempting to linger on the comparison, but our focus here is the biographical work these 19th century forerunners of anthroposophy have recently inspired in non-anthroposophical scholars.

What is so extraordinary about these two biographers, is that they arrive at a picture of their subjects that is so astonishingly true on the basis of conventional scholarly research alone.

Emerson, The Mind On Fire

Rudolf Steiner tells us in the karma lectures that Emerson was the Roman historian Tacitus. Robert D. Richardson, Jr., who wrote *Emerson, The Mind on Fire*,[7] presumably was unaware that Emerson had been Tacitus. Yet so attuned is he to the growth of this powerful thinker, that his entire book documents the picture Rudolf Steiner gives us of Emerson:

> Those who visited Emerson discovered his way of working. There he was in a room; around him were several chairs, several tables. Books lay open everywhere and Emerson walked among them. He would often read a sentence, imbibe it thoroughly, and from it form his own magnificent, free-moving, epigrammatic sentences. That was how he worked. There you have an exact picture of Tacitus in life! Tacitus travels, takes hold of life everywhere; Emerson observes life in *Books.* It all lives again![8]

This is the conclusion to which Richardson comes in his own way. He hits upon this most quintessentially Emersonian attribute and reads not only Emerson's correspondence, diaries, journals, lecture notes, lectures and essays, but also reads and distills everything Emerson read. A formidable task.

When Emerson was fourteen years old and a first year student at Harvard University, his "extracurricular reading was at least three times as extensive as his reading for courses, and he was already in the habit of getting up at 4.30 or 5 in the morning to tend his correspondence and write in his journals."(p.6)

From the first, Waldo not only noted what he read and what he thought of what he read, but what he thought <u>because</u>

of what he read. His journals eventually numbered 236 volumes. They were exquisitely organised, with a system of indexes complete with references and cross-references. "Emerson," writes Richardson, "had a genius for skimming and a comprehensive system for taking notes. Most of the time he was…working his way rapidly through vast mines of material and pocketing the richest bits. He read rapidly, looking for what he could use." (p.67)

Book by book, Richardson elucidates Emerson's learning. We learn why the books were important to Emerson, what Emerson gleaned, what Emerson disregarded, what place these books occupied in their own right, how they related to each other, what others thought of them. Richardson wonderingly chronicles how Emerson read, "to nourish and to stimulate his own thoughts." (p.173)

Tacitus, says Rudolf Steiner, was "a man of wide culture, who knew everything considered worth knowing at that time…" Richardson shows us how Emerson read everything worth knowing, until he, Emerson, was able to transcend the printed wisdom of the past. Richardson documents how, gradually, the great reader, who had been a great writer, became a great writer again. And he well understands that Emerson's reading is striking: "We all read hundreds of books, but the reading does not make us great writers, nor does it very often change our lives […] But the active filtration and the tight focus of constant intention which convert that reading into real life experience and then into adequate expression, these are the exclusive properties of the great writer. "(p.163)

Emerson reached what Richardson calls "prose maturity" (p.179) when he was thirty-one, after 17 years of apprenticeship - to himself. As Tacitus he had written "wonderfully rounded sentences with a genuine epigrammatic ring," says Rudolf Steiner. "Now," comments Richardson, "Emerson can advance the familiar ideas about self-reliance with a fitting language of complete, unarguable conviction [...] The declarative or imperative form of the aphorism presents a discovery in language so taut and trig that the statement is taken for its own evidence."(p.180)

Emerson's thoughts, nourished by his reading, have become so powerful, we might say, so true, that to express himself, he has launched English into a new form. It is Emerson's own image. "I am a rocket manufacturer," he wrote. To which Richardson adds: "He understood early that he 'who can make a good sentence can make a good book.' " (p.202) Richardson realises that, "What he was absorbed in now, and for most of his life, was making sentences. [...] the idea was to use only words that stood for things." (p.205) Thus does the biographer announce Emerson's transcendental realisation that, "The world is emblematic."[9]

Richardson's method, the chronicling of the growth of Emerson's thought life through the tracking of Emerson's huge reading, is an imaginative act capable of revealing the essence of Emerson's genius. Richardson, Emerson's student, absorbs Emerson's truths, and thereby discovers reflections of a karmic truth about Emerson. *Tacitus travels, takes hold of life everywhere; Emerson observes life in Books. It all lives again!*

Yet even apart from this most apt chronicling of the former Roman chronicler, *Emerson, The Mind on Fire* clearly traces the growth of Emerson's vision back to the Roman stoics. Again, two brief references must stand for the many. Describing some journal entries, which would eventually evolve into the great essay, *Nature,* Richardson points out that, "The first three items in this sketch of what would become *Nature* are modern restatements of Stoic thought." (p.152) Later, when Richardson documents the actual writing of *Nature*, he begins a chapter he calls *Nature: The Apocalypse of the Mind,* like this: "The major part of *Nature* explores the relation of Nature to human beings. The Stoics had always maintained that Nature teaches us how to live." (p.230) And early on in the biography, when Emerson is free of the restraints of Academe, and beginning to read in good and earnest, Richardson documents Emerson's plunge into the philosophy of Scottish Common Sense, and its echoes of the Stoics.

Coleridge: Early Visions and Darker Reflections

If we turn our attention now to the Coleridge biography, we find a similar capacity for imaginative empathy for the subject, an empathy which leads to the truth, the poet's truth, the teacher's truth, the anthroposophist's truth, or in this case, the biographer's truth.

Coleridge's biographer, Richard Holmes, not only chronicles Coleridge's developing awareness of truth, he chronicles his own awareness of the awareness.

The biography consists of two volumes. The first volume, published in 1989, is entitled, *Early Visions,* the second, published 9 years later, is called *Darker Reflections.*[10] In the 9 years between these two volumes the biographer himself changed, and recognised that he did so. " I have introduced a series of footnotes," writes Holmes in his preface to the first volume, " which does not so much add information in the traditional scholarly way, as initiate another level of speculation, a third perspective - besides those of Coleridge and his narrator."[11] In other words, this is a way for Holmes to track his own consciousness of consciousness, or as he puts it in the paragraph following the one just quoted, to provide a gloss on "the battle of imagination between subject and biographer."[12] This "battle" is, in reality, the very opposite of conflict, for the biographer delves, with every possible means, into the quarry, the subjects, the Other whom he is pursuing. In an earlier book, *Footsteps*[13], Holmes' tracking of his subjects became as much the focus of his inquiry as the research which he tracked down. One of the subjects of *Footsteps* is Percy Bysshe Shelley. The initial pursuit of the interconnection between Holmes' footsteps, and Shelley's, between Holmes' youthful biography and Shelley's, resulted eventually in Holmes' prize-winning 1974 biography, *Shelley, the Pursuit.*[14] Fourteen years later, the biographer can say of his pursuit of Coleridge that he "has tried to examine his entire life in a broad and sympathetic manner… and above all to make him live, move, talk, and 'have his being.'"[15] It is sympathy wrought to empathy. But by now the biographer places himself outside the frame. The closest he comes to becoming part of the narrative, part of the process of the narrative, apart from the consciousness of the narrative which the author obviously dictates, are the footnotes in which he permits himself the "humble equivalent of Coleridge's marginal 'gloss' to the *Ancient Mariner.*"[16] Holmes' *Footsteps* are now relegated to footnotes. And these footnotes proliferate in volume II.

Out of Holmes' "battle" emerges a character of great power, a character of such power and genius that he <u>and his biographer</u> penetrate the realm of Logos, the realm of the etheric, without a map of spiritual science capable of reaching into the fountainhead of language and thought. Holmes' battle reveals the struggle.

The two processes are inextricable. Consciousness of consciousness depends on the describer even more than on the described. The following excerpt is a fine example of what I mean. Holmes introduces an entry from one of Coleridge's notebooks:

> On 26 November he finally caught the all-night coach for London, and his new career. The following day,

> awakening at dawn, he pulled out his notebook and made a strange, symbolic entry, describing a flock of starlings glimpsed from his carriage window over the low, wintry landscape. 'Starlings in vast flights drove along like smoke, mist, or anything misty without volition - now a circular area inclined in an Arc - now from complete Orb into an Ellipse & Oblong - now a balloon with the car suspended, now a concaved Semicircle - & still it expands & condenses, some moments glimmering & shivering, dim and shadowy, now thickening, deepening, blackening!'

And now comes the extraordinary but characteristically insightful comment by Holmes: "It is an image of shifting energy and imagination; a protean form or a force-field, lacking fixed structure or outline; a powerful personality without a solid identity, or unified will - 'without volition.'"[17]

"An image of shifting energy," of "imagination," "a protean form," a "force field," these are Holmes' words and they clearly describe that which we would call the etheric realm, a realm which Coleridge has unknowingly perceived in the flight of the starlings.

I, too, have watched the flight of great flocks of starlings, along Highway 12 in the Valley of the Moon, north of San Francisco. As a student of anthroposophy, I have "seen" the etheric in the billowing, shifting cloud of birds. For Coleridge, the starlings became emblematic of something to which we can give the name "etheric," Holmes sees it too, and trumps the poetic imagination, but without our concept.

That Coleridge makes the process of the active imagination, the process of creative thinking his field of inquiry, must be acknowledged by any scholar delving into the *Biographia Literaria.* Thus it is not surprising that such a sensitive literary sleuth as Richard Holmes tracks, as his main quarry, the Coleridge imagination, through two thick volumes. Early in the first volume he describes Coleridge's "first attempt to re-invent a poetic world of natural emblems."[18] Later he quotes Coleridge describing his own nature studies: "With my pencil and memorandum book in my hand, I was *making studies,* as the artists calls them, and molding my thoughts into verse, with the objects and imagery immediately before my senses."[19]

Holmes immediately comments: "This process was revolutionary…for Coleridge was now deliberately exploring the technique of making immediate notation made from nature…and which was now steadily intensifying the quality of his vision." In a later comment, Holmes refers to Coleridge's "brilliant series of running *plein-air* sketches, which catch not only the physical sensation of the climber….but also the spiritual effect…"[20] This is insightful stuff because the spiritual effect that a poet or painter can receive while amidst the elements, is of a different quality than that which he can recollect in tranquillity. For Coleridge, tranquillity was a state rarely sought and more rarely achieved. Not for Coleridge that Apollonian state which Wordsworth coined and cultivated. Coleridge's whole biography bespeaks the restless, forceful immersion in sense experience, which he so compellingly captures in words

Later still, to take another from the myriad of possible examples, Holmes quotes Coleridge's description of the River Greta, next to which Coleridge would eventually live: "River Greta near its fall into the Tees - Shootings of water threads down the slope of the huge green stone - The white Eddy-rose that blossom'd up against the stream in the scollop, by fits and starts, obstinate in resurrection - it *is the life* that we live."[21] Again, if you have ever tried to find the words to describe the water that is both steady in its shape, yet constantly reforming itself, you will surely agree that the description is acute. Coleridge is all but naming the etheric -"obstinate in resurrection - it is the life." And Holmes, in a footnote on the facing page expounds on "concepts of a universal Life Force."[22]

In the chapter called "Metaphysical Mountaineer," Holmes further considers Coleridge's fascination with water, and quotes several of Coleridge's amazing descriptions: "The Precipitation of the fallen Angels from Heaven, Flight & Confusion, & Distraction, but all harmonized into one majestic Thing." Writes Holmes: "He was fascinated by the dynamics of the flowing water, and tried to convey the complex appearance of life and deliberate movement: 'The mad water rushed thro' its *sinuous* Bed, or rather prison of Rock, with such rapid Curves, as if it turned the Corners not from the mechanics force, but with foreknowledge, like a fierce and skillful driver...' "Comments Holmes: "Water as usual made him metaphysically aware of the underlying energies of nature, and transcendental implications..."[23]

One feels Coleridge comes up to the very edge of discovering the elemental world *per se.* And one finds Holmes hovering on the brink of Coleridge's consciousness. They are both in the realm of what is, of the "metaphysical," "transcendent" elemental forces of nature - a reality secreted in the very names of the Lake Country waterfalls, which are called "forces," as in Moss Force and Scale Force.

Like Emerson, Coleridge is reading nature, and reading it so penetratingly that he does discover truth. But it is Holmes, like Richardson, who reveals this discovery to us, and does so out of his own discerning vision.

In the second volume of the biography, the biographer is of necessity forced to examine Coleridge's Logos consciousness, for the poet's life culminates in that consciousness. The extent to which Holmes engages this primary field of Coleridge's development as an organizing principle for his biography, is picked up by one of the many rapturous reviews in the English press: "The power of Holmes' portrait...seems to issue from an emotional proximity - and a special proximity to Coleridge's metaphysical tendencies."[24] Holmes telegraphs his proximity to those tendencies with the first sentence of the story it took him fifteen years to write: "Coleridge was always fascinated by anything that promised poetical marvels or metaphysical peculiarities." Whereas Holmes speaks of metaphysical peculiarities, and the reviewers mention metaphysical tendencies, let us not mince words; let us say *Truth,* for what we are pursuing here are the nuggets of truth found by prospectors unaware of what they are finding. (That Holmes is unaware is the immutable pain the anthroposophical reader must experience in the presence of such scholarly brilliance as Holmes achieves; it remains scholarship rather than a deliberate quest for truth. Thus Holmes, in his preface, concludes his list of Coleridge's awesome accomplishments with a summary, but concessionary, "much disputed word - a metaphysician.")

Perhaps the treasure is best viewed directly, though only samples can here be provided. Without furnishing a full-scale gloss on the biography, I can only provide glimpses, and urge my readers to become readers of Holmes and of Coleridge. And as my focus is Holmes rather than Coleridge, I shall quote the biographer rather than the philosopher-poet.

> Thus he stated the central Romantic doctrine…the inwardness of Truth, and its power as a platonic revelation of what exists - or pre-exists - eternally within us. (p.166)[25]

> The notion of the spiritual world, and spiritual longing, being somehow programmed into Nature in an evolutionary sense, was to become of central importance to Coleridge. (p.235)
>
> Truth is the correlative of Being. (p.392)
>
> Coleridge begins to feel his way to a far more subtle picture of the creative mind at work. Here he writes with all the authority of a poet, and finds vivid ways to describe the actual process of sustained mental concentration, "the mind's self-experience in the act of thinking." (p.396)
>
> There was 'no matter without spirit.' (460)
>
> A parallel entry of the final 'Spiritual' section begins with the notion of "wonder" as central to all philosophical thought...(p.540)

Such gleanings are absurd, picked up at random and piled up. The point is that for each of these statements, almost identical words by Rudolf Steiner exist.[26]

To conclude this appreciation of Holmes, I would like to mention that while working on this article, I stumbled unpremeditatedly on a passage by Rudolf Steiner on Coleridge. To my amazement, it occurs in the context of a lecture called, "The Mission of Truth."[27]

"The English poet, Coleridge, once made a statement which can be taken as exemplary for how human beings should relate to truth. He said: Whoever loves Christianity more than truth, will soon see that he loves a Christian sect more than Christianity, and he will see that he loves himself more that his sect. This statement harbors extraordinarily much..."[28] And then Steiner continues to contrast the relationship between the self-love of egoism, and the love that harbors truth.

In our age of political correctness, truth has been bludgeoned. We can only be grateful to such scholars as Holmes and Richardson for their incredible labors of love. Their consciousness of consciousness evolving, is a mighty contribution to our own "battle."

Finding such gleams of truth in scholarly research, particularly in literary biographies, particularly in biographies of those we know to have realized the Living Word, may not be completely surprising, but it is still rare enough to celebrate, for amidst the great sludge of materialistic nonsense choking bookstores, the internet, the multiplex movie theatres, and of course television, such sightings are still few.

They are, however, and that is my thesis here, increasing.

In this vein, allow me one other, seemingly unrelated, phenomenon.

The Media

In the United States, the most credible, least sensational evening news cast, *The NewsHour with Jim Lehrer,* a program of the Public Broadcast Stations (PBS), features a "Media Watch," an occasional journalistic review of journalism, journalists and the media. A web site letter from the "media correspondent" includes the following:

> The mission of the Media Unit at the NewsHour with Jim Lehrer is to report and analyze news, trends, issues and controversies involving the information industries. We cover developments in every medium from the mainstream press and television to alternative media,

> the internet, political and public affairs, advertising and the like. The concept behind this unit is simply this: for better or for worse, we live in an information age. The question of *how people get their news has become a important corollary to the news itself* (italics mine).[30]

The how has become a corollary to the what. The story, in other words, has become the story. Television news, at least this small but significant part of it, has become self-conscious. Thus did the inanity of coverage instigated by the Starr Report lead to recognition of the need for self-knowledge by and of the media. It is an earnest attempt, and in the context of the "information industry," an initiative worth noting.

Becoming conscious of consciousness is a central challenge for the striving of the spiritual scientist. We are enjoined, time and time again, to heighten our sensitivity to process, to stretch our consciousness to include consciousness, to include the subjective in the objective. That the Newshour finds it useful to include such media consciousness of media in its lineup, can only be seen as encouraging.

Let us see ourselves as prospectors of the consciousness soul. Let us notice and support, outwardly, but also inwardly, such precious findings of truth, even by those who do not fully recognise their treasure.

References

1 Quoted in Newsweek, January 11, 1999, p.59, under Science and Technology, in a block headed erasers and delete keys.

2 Rudolf Steiner, *The Mission of Christian Rosenkreutz,* lecture of January 8, 1911.

3 Rudolf Steiner, *Die Mission der neuen Geistesoffenbarung. Das Christus-Eriegneis als Mittelpunktsgeschehen der Erdenevolution.* January 5- December 26, 1911. GA 127.

4 Rudolf Steiner, *The Christian Mystery,* GA 97, lecture of March 8, 1907, Anthroposophic Press, 1998, Hudson, New York. p.65.

5 Rudolf Steiner in *Die Mission der neuen Geistesoffenbarung. Das Christus-Ereigneis als Mittelpunktsgeschehen der Erdenevolution*. GA 127. January 5 - December 26, 1911, p.190 (lecture of June 14, 1911, Vienna). The full sentence and remainder of the paragraph read: "For the theosophical truths are derived from truth itself, they have been fetched down from the great All, they serve the human soul as living nourishment, like bread, like air. If the human being, if humanity, is not to suffocate, if it is to accomplish its mission, this nourishment will have to be brought to it, and indeed, now, because it is so extremely necessary. That is the reason for theosophical study rather than an urge for knowledge, or curiosity, or something possibly even worse." Translated by the author.

6 Rudolf Steiner, *The Christian Mystery,* GA 97, Dec. 11, 1906

7 Robert D. Richardson, *Emerson, The Mind on Fire,* University of California Press, 1995.

8 Rudolf Steiner, Karmic Relationships, vol.2, lecture3, GA 236, April 23, 1924

9 Rudolf Waldo Emerson, in *Nature, Part IV,* see *Ralph Waldo Emerson; Selected Essays, Lectures, and Poems,* ed. by Robert D. Richardson, Jr., Bantam books, 1990

10 Richard Holmes, *Coleridge, Early Visions* Penguin Books, London, 1989; *Coleridge, Darker Reflections,* Harper Collins, London, 1998.

11 Holmes, *Coleridge, Early Visions,* p. xvi

12 Ibid

13 Richard Holmes, Footsteps

14 Richard Holmes, Shelley, the Pursuit

15 Richard Holmes, *Coleridge, Early Visions,* p xiii

16 Ibid, p.xvi.

17 Holmes, *Coleridge Early Visions,* p.254.

18 Ibid, p.51.

19 Ibid, p.161

20 Ibid, p.281

21 Ibid, p.247

22 Ibid. p.246

23 Ibid. p.332

24 James Wood in "The Guardian"

25 Page numbers for this and following references are from volume II, Darker Reflections

26 For example, see my pamphlet *The Art and Science of Teaching Composition* for a detailed examination of Rudolf Steiner on wonder.

27 Rudolf Steiner, GA 58, *Metamorphoses of the Soul,* lecture of October 22, 1909, Berlin. Quotation translated by the author.

28 An endnote to the German edition says the quotation by Coleridge has not been corroborated.

29 Terence Smith, http://www.pbs.org/newshour/media/

Archetypes in Biography

Extracts from a Revised and Extended Lecture
given on 27/01/97

Henning Köhler

Translated from German by William Forward

The following remarks may be regarded as "archetypal" in the sense that they relate to phenomena which seem to apply to everyone equally. Every individual development of the ego in relation to the world is founded on this "model" which provides the framework for individualisation and socialisation. We are not dealing strictly speaking with a "law" but rather with the basic form of the network of relationships between the human being and his environment, the conditions which determine his life, and this basic form will vary with individuals in each case. We shall see how the human being exists on various levels of soul and being, and how one can observe the dynamic of constant shifts from level to level and the continual correspondence of one level with another. Each individual will have his own preferences and one-sidedness - overemphasis or neglect - within this.

What exactly are these levels? The emerging human ego enters the world as what it has become, out of the sphere of the past. In this context we may refer to the level of what is permanent. Initially the human being lives and moves on the level of what is permanent. By this we mean: the world as it has become, what cannot be changed, what is given, i.e. the world of facts. Facts are associated with "down to earth"; one speaks of the facts on the ground, of hard reality. The level of permanence: a world purely of the past. A second major level on which the human being lives is to be found, as it were, between the past and the present. Whilst on the level of permanence we dwell completely in the past, on this level we experience ourselves as beings of the present, but with a strong orientation towards the past. I choose to call this level the level of convention. We are dealing here not so much with facts in the sense of what is established, of "congealed processes", but rather with everything that lives in our environment: it is indeed what is familiar, tried and tested, has been valid for a long time and as such hails from the past, but is also what is constantly being reproduced in the present, being perpetuated by people's customs. On the level of convention we are involved in permanently recurring or unchanging life-processes, social processes, customs, manners, and so on. We meet the world here not simply as hard facts, but find ourselves in a sequence of events (the present); but this pattern of events - like the human beings involved in them - has a strong tendency to persist, a tendency towards uniformity, towards the level of permanence (the past). One can summarise this as a level which primarily belongs to the past but which inserts itself into the present in the form of convention.

We are however not confined to these two levels in our relation to the world, but can emancipate ourselves from both when we fully enter the world of the present, the level which is also open towards the future: where the human being is at play. The human being at play - "homo ludens" - in the sense described by Friedrich Schiller or also by Joseph Beuys, who derived his concept of the human as artist from Schiller's "urge to play", makes the present receptive to what is surging in towards it from the future. As players and dancers, as impulsive, flighty beings related to the element of air we are living on the level of transformation. This is the level of effortless metamorphosis, of teeming fantasy, of creative freedom, but also the level of confusion, inconstancy and lack of orientation.

The fourth level I shall refer to as the level of revolt or new creation. This is the level on which the human being always feels the urge to start from scratch, to reinvent himself. Thus the term "revolt" is used here not in the sense of overthrowing some outer institution (though this may well be allied to the impulse to start afresh), but rather in the sense of emancipation from what has already completed its process of becoming. Rudolf Steiner spoke of how the human ego, the "I", the core of the human being tends to revolt against the world as it has become. We find ourselves fundamentally at odds with the forces of the past, the forces also of the periphery: forces which, as Steiner puts it, "create one's life-situation" and "maintain one's life-situation", and thus determine us and, as it were, pollute our own creative intentions. The creative human being rejects all this. Steiner even uses the terms "paralyse" and "eliminate". This is the level on which the CHILD is at home, the unique child in each of us. I am aware that my choice of words might seem strange - the juxtaposition of "CHILD" and "revolt" - but the birth of a child is after all the most revolutionary process one can imagine and the rebirth of the CHILD in the midst of life (for instance when you find the courage in a seemingly stuck situation to experiment, to forge new plans, to begin something new, to wonder, to ask, to seek, to change yourself) may also be termed a form of upheaval: a creative breach of the continuity. The fact that human beings come to Earth at all, that we all took the resolve for this life we are living, each one of us with unprecedented impulses, with astonishing power of hope, with an unfathomable will for renewal - this is revolutionary. Thus to the extent that one has remained the "CHILD" one is living on the level of revolt or new creation. But now we must pause for thought: on the level of new creation the human being is also a suffering being, one who suffers/endures the world, for throughout his life he will not succeed in feeling at home on the Earth, let alone feel "good" and in harmony with the world (as all the so-called life style experts would have us be today). Anyone who wishes to be "constantly in harmony with himself and with the world" must somehow silence the "CHILD", which of necessity is creatively dissatisfied, and this is a high price to pay. On the level of new creation it is not least we ourselves who bring suffering upon ourselves. It is one of the laws of biography that every single human being turns from the refuge of the undamaged child nature within him against what has come to be in his life, constantly wishes to eliminate it with a destructive impulse, if you like, and thus causes himself pain. The human condition includes a self-destructive, patently auto-aggressive tendency, and this is no death wish (Thanatos) but an urge to liberate himself. In extreme cases this may lead to someone ruining the foundations of his existence out of a kind of biographical fear of death. Thus the generally unconscious urge to "paralyse" what has come to completion is inevitable, and despite its antipathetic rejecting gesture towards the world, it is in its essence productive. It can however be misunderstood and misdirected if it finds itself in a life situation which seems to offer no opportunity for creativity. After all we are speaking of a force which is not merely antipathy but contains within it the urge to break up and remould the biography as it has been. Please do not misunderstand me: next to this "urge for new creation" there is also an urge to sustain, to conserve, and it is clear that what lies in the past, must, in the end, be integrated, be given its meaning within the whole. But if we look at the various levels of being and at their characteristic gestures, then on the level of revolt or new creation the following is true: the

CHILD rebels, must rebel against outside interference, excessive form, limitations or restrictions imposed on its primary intentions. Coming to yourself must also mean: raging against anything from outside which forms, restricts or imposes conditions, against the veneer of the past and the force of circumstance, and it does not really matter a great deal whether such circumstances are comfortable or uncomfortable. Thus the human being as an ego-being has the tendency to tear himself loose from his surroundings and to react with hostility towards anything within or around himself which he cannot recognise as truly his own. On the other hand this hostile reaction may also lead to a creative tension by means of the alchemy of an artistic approach to one's own biography and the ennobling of one's "base metals" by the forces of the future.

Let us now take a closer look at these four aspects, beginning with the first, the level of "hard reality". For the being of spirit and soul who enters the physical plane, this physical plane is indeed "hard reality". Moreover each of us carries with us on our journey through life a piece of this "hard reality", namely our physical body, to which we are bound for good or ill. I "inhabit" a physical body which consists in the first place of hard material substance, secondly of fluids, thirdly is permeated by air, and fourthly is filled with warmth. It is thus composed of the four elements like a "little Earth". As incarnate beings we are directly, existentially and unavoidably bound up with the facts of earthly existence. Permanence: this is physicality as such; this is the genetic predisposition with which we have to live; it is the surface of the Earth on which we stand and walk, held firmly by gravity; it is Nature around us, whether in pristine condition or transformed by humankind; everything which, whether as divine creation or human creation, provides the framework for our existence, regardless of our will or our agreement; which is simply there whether we like it or not, and which leaves us no freedom of choice. Metaphorically what corresponds to this in our biography is the past: what has happened cannot be undone. The world as it has become. If we draw a comparison from the four elements in terms of their significance, - or, to borrow a phrase from Goethe's theory of colour, in terms of their sense-perceptible and moral essence - we may regard the level of permanence as comparable to the mineral world. You might prefer to call it a symbolic association. "Stone" stands for materiality, hardness, objectivity, lifelessness, something that has been, but also of course for reliability, security, load-bearing capacity and majestic calm. We feel the world of inalterable facts to be like the mineral world in both the positive and negative senses, even when we are dealing with facts in the mind. Thus the human being has on the level of permanence to deal with the physical and quasi-physical facts and both these can be related to the qualities of the mineral world and to gravity. The young child finds its way into this sphere as it explores the world through the sense of touch. In this way it becomes familiar with the surface of things, with structure and form with the world of objects and objectivity as such: with the principle of matter. This entering into relation with the "substantiality of the world" (Rudolf Steiner) through the sense of touch dominates the child's development in its first 3-4 years of life. Other things happen in these years, many others, but the development of the sense of touch is the principle theme. In this way the foundations are laid for trust in life and security within one's body. The latter for the reason that one's primary experience through the sense of touch is of one's own body: the perception of the boundary defined by one's skin. The searching activity of reaching out to touch something leads to a sense of reality. The other side of the coin is the painful experience of bumping into things; the child learns to know the rugged impenetrability, rigidity and sheer bulk of matter as a form of rejection and a kind of elemental curtailment of its freedom. It has to come to terms with the difficulty of existence. The resultant frustration contributes to the triggering of early tantrums.

So the human being is consolidated as a being of permanence in the first few years of life. They are spent in becoming familiar with the objectivity of the world - and, it must be remembered in connection with "materiality" - in properly developing the child's bone structure. If as an adult one does not feel fully "grounded" in this element, which is becoming increasingly common, if a fundamental sense of security is lacking in your constitution, so that you are constantly beset by the feeling that you are on shaky ground and cannot rely on the firm, stable uncontestable existence of things, even of your own body, then you should direct your attention to the first 3-4 years of your life to find out what is wrong. There does not necessarily have to be a simple causal relationship (experience x missing in early childhood leads to complication y in adulthood), since even if development took place under ideal conditions the outcome is by no means secured for all time. Quite the contrary: everything which we have once acquired can slip from our grasp again and this applies in matters of soul development just as it does for outer things, every biographical achievement has at some time or other to undergo a testing process. I have heard quite a number of people complain thus , "I am somehow not sure of where I stand, I don't feel secure in my own body; it is as if I were walking on thin ice; when I look at, or touch quite ordinary things I ask myself, "Is it reality? Does it really exist? Do I really exist?" This mood is described primarily in cases of non-specific anxiety. There are cases where this can increase to the point of severe confusion, but generally it is only a latent condition and can be more or less balanced out in everyday life. I maintain that almost everyone has had some experience of this. When it creeps up on you, you have a strange sense of unreality; you feel the urge to do something to confirm that you do exist and that everything else does too. Where this occurs and develops into a chronic problem we are dealing with a complication which can only be understood if one can re-establish a link with the early childhood experience of feeling one's way into the world. This is where guidelines may be found for therapeutic access to such anxiety-ridden conditions where the sense of reality is blurred; processes have to be stimulated where this developmental stage can be recapitulated. This is where the therapist is called upon to be an artist, for nothing can be achieved by mere prescriptions. One has to grasp the connections in the whole process of human development and then develop ideas appropriate to the individual concerned. Someone who is too loosely connected with reality, and is anxious that he is not on firm ground (which is always accompanied by an inadequate sense of security in relation to his own past, i.e. inability to identify fully with the course of his life so far) needs to establish a better connection to his own body and his own past, to develop a productive relationship to the principle of "matter" both literally and metaphorically, to bring order into the world of his memories, to practice exact observation, to develop concrete mental images, to practice the perceiving of form and structure. These guidelines might also help a counsellor who is trying by means of conversation to develop practical suggestions on how to implement changes in the patient's life. The same applies to the usually highly desirable co-option of physiotherapy, movement or artistic therapies in the process of managing the crisis. Likewise doctors who understand the relationship between natural processes and the elements of the human being may translate the idea of "anchoring in reality" into appropriate medicaments.

In addition to people who are insufficiently anchored in reality there are of course also those who suffer from the opposite condition, namely that of being, as it were, riveted to what is material and physical. Typically such a person might be somewhat heavy in his whole way of being, inflexible, laborious in manner, inclined to hate all changes (especially unforeseen ones), crassly oriented towards the past in all matters of opinion, habit and preference, someone who misses no opportunity to praise former and better times, who collects all manner of worthless old things, who constantly wishes to go over old holiday photos and suspiciously guards his belongings. Such a person might seek help because he no longer takes pleasure in life, but finds everything terribly grey, feels himself surrounded by people who have no respect for the tried and tested values of the past, becomes increasingly melancholy and only does his daily work out of a sense of duty, then relapsing into silent brooding. With sufficient empathy one can recognise in this excessive attachment to the past a remarkable quality. If the person concerned is able make positive use of his disposition then he will shine as someone who is reliable, thoughtful, circumspect and the best possible sanctuary for anyone who needs to feel secure in a time of anxiety. This confidence-inspiring nature has only been obscured by the fact that for one reason or another the other levels on which the ego relates to the world have become less accessible to him. The corrective qualities of "conventional" adaptability, of going with the flow, but also of "transformative" playfulness are lacking, and so it happens that no creative impulses from the uppermost "ego level" come through leaving only a grumpy sense of alienation from the world. Indeed, if one is too firmly grounded in practical life that in itself can lead to a kind of loss of reality. The positive aspects of the grounded, conservative nature can only be brought to bear if it is balanced by the activity of the other levels of convention, transformation and creativity. It thus becomes the task of the therapist to stimulate a corresponding process of harmonisation. It might, for example, involve getting the client to do free, or abstract artistic compositions either sculpturally or in colour, acquainting him with the nature of colours, developing a sense for processes, for what evolves and metamorphoses in the stream of time (perhaps by encouraging exercises in movement) or indeed looking at the person's biography with just these qualities. It would be important to draw his attention to the fact that he may have completely forgotten how to listen attentively. These are merely pointers in the direction of where a therapist might look for inspiration. They could equally be applied to a critical self-examination.

Now, whereas the level of permanence is altogether bound up in the past, the level of convention I have characterised is an intermediary level between the past and the present. This is where we are creatures of habit, social beings, embedded into traditional ways of life, mores and customs: into everything around us which is continuity, regular recurrence, repetitive process. There is nothing fixed on this level but it is a sequence of recurring events based on firm rules or rhythmic cycles. The quality of permanence dissolves into this level as something living and moving. The archetype for this is actually to be found in Nature: sunrise and sunset, the seasons, blossoming and withering, growth and decline. To the extent that a human being is a being of convention (in the sense we are using) he imitates the processes of Nature. The conventions we find in cultural or social life might likewise be termed communal imitation of Nature. Thus we profit from the wisdom of Nature by incorporating similar rhythms and processes into our culture, and find support and orientation in them. Traditions, customs and rituals - humanity has always had rituals, they are indispensable - have the effect of giving orientation, security (they reduce anxiety) and integration. On the other hand it is also quite possible simply to sink into this rhythmic security. The danger is that we give ourselves up too strongly to convention: an excessive adaptability that results in us not feeling ourselves as individuals sufficiently clearly or not bringing our individuality to light. If a person suffers from this one-sidedness he becomes dependant and uncritical, perhaps with a tendency to opportunism. The need to be normal, to conform, to be part of a social grouping and secure in a regular pattern of life can take over and obscure what is independent, original, unique in the person concerned. Critics would describe such a person as a "hanger-on" or "a notorious yes-man", who "doesn't know where he stands". This condition is often also accompanied by the tendency to anxiously ward off anything strange or unfamiliar. On the other hand the extremely conventional type might react with great distress and sadness if, for example, a social custom which has gone on regularly for years, - a feast, a ceremony, a gathering - is suddenly cancelled or completely altered. Unlike the previous case, the person who is trapped in convention is a highly convivial, gregarious person, often even the "life and soul of the party" so long as everything continues as usual. The worst thing for this type is being alone. He cannot occupy himself. His hobbies and interests are entirely geared to social activity (unlike the "guardian of the past" for whom things are often more important than people), his moods are to a great extent determined by his surroundings. He cannot join a social activity and remain himself. He lacks the necessary capacity to set boundaries. He cannot understand people who stand back although he himself might appear very shocked the moment something turned out to be not exactly as expected. He is utterly faithful and attentive and others appreciate his considerate, helpful manner. Anyone living with him would however have to beware of introducing any kind of new-fangled ideas or changes to the order of daily life. These make him frightened and then he can be unpredictable. He cannot stand any kind of extravagance. He enjoys wearing fine clothes and looking well-groomed (this also distinguishes him from the "guardian of the past" who prefers to always wear the same old baggy trousers) but the status quo must always be maintained. On no account does he wish to stand out in the crowd.

This again somewhat caricatured description of an excessive commitment to the level of convention highlights a constitution that is inclined to pay devoted attention to and imitate what is going on in its social surroundings: "What are conditions like? How can I adapt to them, fit in?" What is exaggerated in such a person? Essentially it is the soul's imitation of water. Water is the element which adapts to all forms. The two hallmarks of the liquid element are: firstly its tendency to flow, and secondly its propensity to adapt to all given forms. There we have the archetype for the "conventional" quality. Just as the human being on the level of permanence is earthbound, so on the level of convention he is a water being. In this area we have an imitative relationship to the world. Thus if we are once again seeking guidelines for dealing with conflicts which have to do with a one-sidedness on the level of convention and look back to childhood experiences, then we are bound to be interested in the phase of development where imitation is pre-eminent and where actually everything is based on imitative learning. This is the time roughly between the child's fourth or fifth and ninth years. In these years the unconscious imitation of gesture gradually passes over into the imitation of habits of language, thought and life, of customs and rituals in the environment and at the same time it is the phase in which the child masters the element of water in its physical and soul development. When, as an adult, over-emphasis of the principle of convention becomes a problem, and when there is a danger that the creative individual will get lost on this level, then the person concerned will in principle have to recapitulate the phase of development he went through between the ages of five and eight in order to regain his autonomy. If all went well, he will at that time, as it were, have tamed the "water-being within him" and have learned to control his urge to imitate to such an extent that it became possible (at that time still in a child-like way) to act out of his own free creative impulses. Do not imagine for a moment that it is not necessarily painful to be excessively oriented to one's surroundings, to be adaptable to the extent of self-obliteration! From a certain point on those concerned experience great fear, namely when they become so one-sided that they are no longer able to validate the positive aspects of their disposition and feel that they are gradually losing their identity. This can lead to dangerous feelings of emptiness of soul, powerlessness and helplessness. In some cases it is a predisposition that was always present and has somehow become distorted, in others it is more a consequence of some experience of failure, fear or extreme loneliness that pushes them in this direction, which actually does not really correspond to their nature but, once established, seems impossible to shake off. Then, of course, there is also the "complementary" type who finds it impossible to function adequately on the level of convention, who can fit in nowhere, who constantly drops out of group processes: the person who is compulsively unable to adapt, who is alone in the world and can find no home, neither in a given place or among a given group of people, neither in any form of culture, nor indeed even within himself. He has much in common with the person who has gone astray on the level of transformation.

What does it mean, to have gone astray on the level of transformation? This is where we said the human being dances, where he is a changeable, fickle being, a butterfly, and this is a quality that we also need in sufficient quantity if we are to be able to act creatively within our own biography. This is the level of the lightning decision, where we can move in a trice, can react flexibly, only touching on things lightly, playing with them, experimenting, following our curiosity, dancing; where we grow wings, where we are related to the wind. The phase of child development that corresponds to the transformative soul disposition (in which there is constant change, hopping from one thing to another, delighting in movement) is the time between the 9th and 12th years. In this phase the child acquires a mastery of the airy element, on the one hand consolidating its capacity for movement and on the other attaining maturity in its breathing processes in both soul and body. "The sensation of one's own, free soul-life" (Rudolf Steiner, on the sense of movement) which can be kindled by guided, "beautiful" movement, becomes an elixir of life. The allocation of the "level of transformation" to the middle of childhood is by no means contradicted by the fact that moments of loneliness and sadness also play an important role in the years from nine to twelve, since there are dark zones on all four levels, and that applies to the four developmental stages in childhood too. Within the airy, flighty, butterfly-like element there lurks the danger of non-committal rootlessness, lonely erring about, homelessness. If the windy, spiralling tendency becomes too strong there is chaos. The one-sidedly developed transformation type is afraid of ever arriving, staying and putting down roots. He is afraid of persevering. He is afraid of binding intimacy. He inclines towards unfaithfulness and yet is constantly seeking warmth and security. Wherever he may end up: he has to say goodbye before he has properly arrived. The sorrow of parting becomes the basic melody of his life, yet he cannot change it, the addition of uncertainty constantly lures him away. This does not only apply to people and places but to "inner farewells": from ideas, convictions, plans, interests. To begin with this sorrow is relatively mild. His butterfly nature helps him to quickly turn to something new. However over time the constant breaking off of connections wears him down, the feeling of being alone and lost condenses, and eventually the harum-scarum is no longer flying about but dragging himself from place to place. To help someone out of this type of one-sidedness one has to lead him towards the level of permanence, in such a way that he discovers its materiality, its malleability and learns to value the support that it can offer him without becoming afraid of turning into stone. It is important that he reconcile himself to the principle of work (work = deploying energy and time in relation to the pliancy of the material that has to be formed). He must also recognise the advantages of the level of convention, such as the healing power of rituals, the value of faithfulness (by which I do not only mean faithfulness to other people but also in the broadest sense faithfulness to one's tasks), and to feel that being at home does not necessarily have to mean the same as being imprisoned.

Only when the extreme "transformation type" is willing to correct his false conception of freedom and lack of restraint can the "new creator" who wishes to creatively take hold of his material, do so without constantly grasping at thin air. Being lost in the moment from one situation to the next, without reference to a context and with no foundations, above all with no perspective on the future - this is like a wicked spell. The complementary type to this is the pedant, the obsessive, the martinet, the fanatic on form and order, who has a fetish for form and order and stubbornly perseveres with projects although deep in his heart he is very unhappy because he can neither freely enjoy anything nor give himself up to undirected playfulness. (He does of course remind us of the type who was riveted to reality and yet the two are not quite the same). What this type needs is "the human sense of freedom that allows him to experience himself as a soul-being" (Rudolf Steiner) which is imparted by the sense of movement. Not that he lacks a rich and deep soul-life. The problem is that in the "planning office" of his everyday life he can hardly perceive it any longer. It is therefore all the more important that there are at least one or two people around him who can let him feel that they genuinely value his qualities. Then he may succeed in the truest sense of the word in making a virtue out of necessity. For this type of being also bears within it qualities which are needed in the world! What use are the most beautiful creative impulses and the most idealistic goals, if there is no-one there with the organisational talent to implement them, who can ensure there is order and clarity in the planning phase? Anyone who has failed to develop qualities of perseverance and thoroughness within himself - at least to some extent - or who cannot find a companion to replace this lack in himself will never be able to realise his ideals, however shining they might be. The conclusion is that a person can be either too much or too little involved on the level of transformation and both forms of one-sidedness have to do with the fact that the four component parts of the biographical archetype do not interrelate adequately

It is on the fourth level, that of revolt or new creation, that the human being is closest to his core, adjoined to the refuge of the CHILD within him. This fourth level is itself divided into four distinct elements: The "I become" (1), the asker of the question (2), the seeker (3) and the shaper (4). We may speak here of the sphere of aims or freely-formed intentions, but also of the sphere of the fiery will, the will for renewal, for shaping ideals, the will that is also wrath: not blind rage, but the kind of anger that plays a part in every creative impulse and which is directed at the sclerotic tendencies which oppose the creative will; against established habits, against the firmly ensconced status quo, time grown old. Often it is a sense of moral outrage that moves us at this level, a flaring up against any encroachment on freedom. Within that there is always an ethical or aesthetic concern at work. In our revolt against what has come from the past we are on the one hand citizens of the Earth (drawing on the forces of youth that we have been able to sustain) and on the other we are connected to that mysterious region where the CHILD watches over the original creative impulse with which we embarked on our journey of life. To the extent that the level of revolt reaches into this world, i.e. into our earthbound consciousness, there can be aberrations on this level, just as there were on the other three: aberrations in two directions. The power that rays out from this level can prove violent and destructive on the level of permanence, when for instance the impulse does not take with it the element of fantasy from the transformation level and is not, as it were, braked a little on the level of convention to acquire a sense for form (a living sense for form!). At the other extreme, obviously, it can be that the will for new creation is too weak for various reasons. We have encountered such soul conditions in our consideration of the other levels.

Thus we have before us in outline the fourfold biographical archetype, the archetypal composition of the biographical gestalt. This picture is one that one keeps in mind when someone else asks for advice and support in order to gain a first basic impression of their soul constitution. The question is always: at what point, on what level, in which transition area between one level and another is the client who is seeking for the sources of his being (everyone is seeking the source of their being throughout their lives, it is just that this becomes obvious in a crisis) blocked, misled or discouraged? Where and how is the connection to the inner CHILD interrupted? Can this be characterised more precisely? If one works with the biographical archetype over a period of time then one can as a counsellor identify the basic tendencies by means of these concepts in the course of a series of investigative conversations. Later on the individuality with its own unique impulses will come increasingly to the fore, but one has first to work one's way through to the level of new creation and to the yearning that lives there.

Published in abridged translation by kind permission of 1998 GESUNDHEITSPFLEGE initiator, gemeinnutzige Bildungrgesellschaft mbH Esslingen.

A Reluctant Autobiographer

Doré Deverell

When I went to Europe in 1997 to speak about my book, *Light Beyond the Darkness, The healing of a Suicide Across the Threshold of Death,* I knew I would find a part of me that I had never met. And I did. Only because I did, have I considered writing an autobiography, and then, only insofar as it is spiritually relevant.

I didn't even consider that my first book, *How I Healed My Cancer Holistically (1976),* was autobiographical. I had overcome cancer through my own research without surgery, radiation or chemotherapy. I wanted to share that with other people so they could do the same. I wrote about my overcoming cancer more as an isolated incident in my life. Indeed, it was as if I was writing about some one else.

When my son committed suicide in 1982 and I found anthroposophy in 1983, at age 60, I learned that I could help him by reading anthroposophy to him. I did this for seven years which changed my life and his in the spiritual worlds. During this time, I was asked when I was going to write a book about reading to the dead. I knew this was a destiny question so I wrote *Light Beyond the Darkness* to help people who had loved ones who had committed suicide and the suicides themselves. Most importantly, I wanted to try to prevent suicides by sharing that the suffering of a suicide after death is far worse than their suffering in life before death.

I tried to hide myself in that book; I endeavoured to

describe my son's life as if he had grown up in a vacuum. This was impossible, of course, but I told as little as possible about myself.

To be honest, I was ashamed of my life. I had been an alcoholic. I felt like a failure as a mother. I had always had problems with relationships. After I left my marriage of 27 years, no matter how hard I tried, I seemed incapable of establishing a permanent home or place in the world for myself: I couldn't bear to work at something that was meaningless to me, but I couldn't support myself doing what I liked because I didn't have the proper credentials. I did, however, have a knack for counselling, teaching classes and workshops, and lecturing about holistic health subjects because of my experience with overcoming cancer.

I even went back to college to try to get a credential, but I couldn't bear what they were teaching. Most of it seemed irrelevant to me and I was already in my 50s.

I started getting inklings that my life might have some value when a young man who helped me with *Light* saw my experiences of reading to my son from an esoteric viewpoint, and I moved from the personal to the supra personal view of my relationship with my son which had been so painful when he was alive.

Next, my spiritual teacher, a very wise anthroposophist, was deeply touched by my son's story and encouraged me to write about it. He also said to me, "Now, don't you feel guilty; the spiritual world takes us through the most incredible darkness before we come to the light."

When Temple Lodge Publishing wanted to publish *Light,* I was totally surprised. I would never have sent the manuscript there except for the most astonishing, miraculous circumstances that led me to do so.

In 1996, the year *Light* was published, I met a clairvoyant anthroposophist whose works I had been studying. He had read *Light* and liked it. In a private conversation he said, "What you have to give to the world is alcoholism, cancer and suicide."

I said, "Oh, no, I would much rather teach *Knowledge of Higher Worlds*. I don't want to think about those experiences any more."

But I knew he was right. So I started writing a booklet "Finding a Greater Good in the Greatest Evils: Alcoholism, Cancer and Suicide." I gave several workshops on the subject in Holland, Germany and England. Temple Lodge liked to booklet and asked me to expand it into a book about overcoming alcoholism and cancer and its esoteric significance in my life as a companion to the suicide book. I agreed to do so because by this time I had met that part of me that was hidden before.

In Holland I learned about the "other Michael stream" which Ita Wegman refers to in the Introduction of her book, *On the Work of Michael,* where one follows the path of evil without becoming evil. I was deeply moved by this knowledge. Then in Germany I was read an article by Gerhard von Beckerath in *"Was in der Anthroposophischen Gesellschaft Vorgeht,"* September 1991, about the two Michael streams. He characterizes two streams down through the ages starting with Cain and Abel. The Abel stream works from above downward and the Cain stream works from below upwards. The stream gains wisdom from working on the earth. I identified strongly with this earthly stream.

Then my hostess in Germany who had been to my workshop said: " You seem to have these difficult experiences so you can write about them to help others."

Another confirmation I received on my tour was the warm, enthusiastic response from people who were eager to hear about experiential anthroposophy. This was heartwarming because sharing personal spiritual experiences is rare in my community. My belief is that the more personal something is the more universal it is. How wonderful it was to have this confirmed by many people in all of the countries I visited. Many of these people shared their experiences with me that they had never shared with anyone before.

When Temple Lodge asked me to write the next book, I knew that I would have to reveal more than I had before, but now I was able to realize, that the only thing I had to give to the world were these experiences and how, through finding anthroposophy, I finally could understand the meaning of them. (This book will be published in Spring 2000.)

However, when I tried to write about alcoholism and cancer, I realize that I had to start with the abuse and stunted development I experienced as a child that set the tenor of the rest of my life.

I started with my birth and organized information from journals and my research over the years to the present (I am now 75). The journals and other files included therapy sessions and writings of my own inner work from the beginning of my search for healing, which began when I entered Alcoholics Anonymous when I was 46. I had much material which I had collected over the years.

The research included 15 years of intensive study of Rudolf Steiner and other anthroposophical authors such as Bernard Lievegoed's *Man on the Threshold, Phases of Childhood, Phases;* Jocelyn Beredene's *Citizen of the Cosmos,* Georg Kühlewind's *From Normal to Healthy,* and others. I pieced together a description of why I experienced my life as I had.

I learned that because of the experiences of my first three years of life, I have carried a depression of spirit during my entire lifetime as characterized in Rudolf Steiner's

Manifestations of Karma, page 76. Moreover, my childhood and adolescence were continuously negative, full of rejection, abusive, undermining and belittling. My relationships with my family demanded that I need nothing and take care of everyone else. Of course, everyone experiences such things to some degree. However, my situation was extreme.

We lived at my grandmother's house until I was three and she hated me. My mother told me that my father wouldn't leave me alone with Granny because she was so cruel to me.

I came into a dark, cold, hostile world. I discovered it wasn't safe to need anything. In addition to emotional traumas, my mother told me she had not allowed me to crawl because she didn't want me to get dirty. I learned in Jean Ayres *Sensory Integration and the Child,* that this alone causes great handicaps: the brain doesn't develop properly which causes learning difficulties, insecurities and emotional problems which can't be treated psychologically, but can only be remedied through sequential movement therapy.

My mother was a very disturbed woman. She had been horribly abused during her childhood by both parents and this spilled over in crazy behaviour at stressful times in her life. For example, she pretended to be dead on two different occasions, once when I was between two and three years old which she told me about. The one I remember was when I was 11 years old. I found her lying on the floor near a gas stove. I ran over to her crying, "Mom, Mom."

She sat up laughing and said, "I just wanted to know if you love me." I became hysterical.

As a young adult I was totally unconnected from other people until I was 57 when my first grandson was born. I was filled with confusion, despair and self-hate. I became addicted to cigarettes, coffee, sugar and alcohol. I couldn't understand why I had such difficulty with relationships. When I married I had no pleasure in love making, and experienced no joy with my children. According to Bernard Lievegoed's work, these emotional reactions are all too common in today's world and the result of childhood traumas and stunted development.

On the other hand, there were many moments of light that carried me through. My mom taught me to pray and to think about Christ as if he were present. She referred to him as "The Good Lord", and mentioned him often. So, parallel with my depressed, negative feelings about myself, fear and distrust of people, and floating anger at the world, when I was 16 I started my spiritual search and have been pursuing it since.

In 1964, at age 40, I had a spiritual experience in the middle of my life's darkest years, 1962 - 1969, to which I clung. I didn't understand this experience fully. I also couldn't understand how I could have such an experience and still slide further into the abyss. I meditated and journal-wrote for years on this experience and received only a few inklings during that time. The mystery was solved 33 years later in Europe when I heard about the "other Michael stream" which I mentioned earlier. I had known, of course, about the Manichean stream, but I had no idea how that manifested in everyday life.

Slowly my experiences started to come together to form a coherent picture. I asked myself, "Does not my personal life reflect what society universally is going through today: child abuse, addictions, divorce, cancer, suicide? Can my life show others that a greater good can be found by going through these evils?" In the forthcoming book I will share in detail how I overcame them and found a greater good. Here, I do so briefly.

In Alcoholics Anonymous I experienced unconditional love for the first time and found my first tools to apply to life's situations. I learned to admit my powerlessness and to depend on the power of God, to make an inventory of my life and to take responsibility for it and to blame no one, to make amends to others, to forgive others, to help others, to pray and meditate, and to try to practise these principles in my life. These 12 steps are spiritual steps, indeed, and are a great gift to the consciousness soul age.

Then I had to face cancer. In that experience, I learned that I had no identity as a person. My ego had been beaten down by child abuse, submerged by the alcohol and totally eclipsed by the prescription drugs a psychiatrist had prescribed for years. I was slowly emerging through working the 12 steps. However, cancer needed quicker, more drastic changes. I had to change my lifestyle, quicken the process of healing emotional traumas, use my mind to visualize healing the cancer and to change my thoughts to positive ones. My ego was tremendously strengthened by taking hold of my healing and by refusing to go along with conventional medicine, which I thought barbaric in its treatment of cancer. I had not yet found anthroposophical medicine.

Even my son's suicide turned out to be the greatest blessing in my life. Through it I was led to anthroposophy, and through reading anthroposophy to him, I was able to help him to move from a place of dark despair in the spiritual worlds to a place filled with light where he could see everything. Then, to my amazement, after seven years of reading, I feel that he was able to return to earth in a new incarnation enriched by hearing over 2,000 anthroposophical lectures. My son's life and my relationship to him are a mystery still unrevealed.

Through anthroposophy, of course, came knowledge of the spirit. I learned that I had a strong spirit but a parched, compressed soul. I attended Rudolf Steiner College for five years taking the Foundation Year, the Teacher Training and three years of the Arts Program. I found the anthroposophical therapies to heal my soul and body. I enthusiastically joined the Anthroposophical Society and worked diligently in the branch.

I joined several study groups in addition. What a relief it was to have found my place at last!

My child abuse, the last to be understood, but the first to be experienced in this life, gave my great sensitivity to and understanding of others and myself. I learned to forgive and have compassion for my abusers, and finally could forgive myself for my inability to love unconditionally those many years. Sergei O. Prokofieff in *The Occult Significance of Forgiveness,* tells us that forgiveness lessens karmic necessity and replaces it with grace. One can help ease the karma of another and one's self by forgiving!

Though many mysteries still remain, I believe that I chose these experiences to overcome as much karma as possible and to strengthen my ego so I can do more and better work sooner next time.

The task of the fifth post-Atlantean epoch is to confront evil. Rudolf Steiner says in *From Symptom to Reality in Modern History,* p. 112, "By a strange paradox mankind is led to a renewed experience of the Mystery of Golgotha in the fifth epoch through the forces of evil. Through the experience of evil it will be possible for the Christ to appear again, just as he appeared in the fourth post-Atlantean epoch through the experience of death."

Arising out of what I have shared here, which is work in progress, these are the thoughts that I am using now to help shape my perception as I look out into the world:

In Christ we die to find life.

In Christ we learn to confront evil so we can choose the good in freedom, which leads us to His Love.

References

Ayres, A. Jean, Ph.D., *Sensory Integration and the Child,* Western Psychological Services, 12031 Wilshire Blvd., Los Angeles, CA 90025. 1979.
Beredene, Jocelyn, *Citizens of the Cosmos,* Continuum Publishing Company, 575 Lexington Avenue., New York 10022.
Kühlewind, Georg, *From Normal to Healthy,* Lindisfarne Press, 195 Main Street., Great Barrington, MA, 01230, 1988.
Lievegoed, Bernard, *The Battle for the Soul,* Hawthorn Press, Stroud, Glos, GL5 1BJ, 1993.
Lievegoed, Bernard, *The Eye of the Needle,* Hawthorn Press, Stroud, 1993
Lievegoed, Bernard, *Man on the Threshold,* Hawthorn Press, Stroud, 1985
Lievegoed, Bernard, *Phases,* Rudolf Steiner Press, Bristol, 1993
Lievegoed, Bernard, *Phases of Childhood,* Floris Books, Edinburgh EH11 1SH, 1997
Prokofieff, Sergei O., *The Occult Significance of Forgiveness,* Temple Lodge Press, London, 51 Queen Caroline Street, London W6 9QL, 1991
Steiner, Rudolf, *From Symptom to Reality in Modern History,* Rudolf Steiner Press, London, 1976
Steiner, Rudolf, *The Manifestations of Karma,* Rudolf Steiner Press, London, 1969

Telling Encounters

Mathias Wais

Translated from German by William Forward

This is not intended as an overview of what Rudolf Steiner had to say on this subject, but is rather drawn from my experience of working with individuals and couples whose relationships have got into a state of crisis. I have observed the progress of encounters and relationships and am attempting to draw conclusions on the basis of a spiritual image of the human being, quite conscious that there are limits to my powers of insight into the situations I describe.

Secondly, I should like to urge that we approach this theme with a certain calmness, thoroughness and discretion as opposed to heightened and perhaps exaggerated expectations: if we already start out with a spiritual image of the human being, then we should find it neither unusual nor surprising that a large number of our encounters and relationships arise out of the karma of those concerned. If the essence of the human being is of a spiritual nature, i.e. it exists independently of its physical clothing, then it goes without saying that it will take on such clothing again and again, and will seek ever new constellations of encounter in order to further its development. It is equally obvious that the possibilities latent in an earthly encounter or relationship may not be exhausted in the course of one earthly life. Thus a yearning, indeed a will must arise, to take up again what could not be achieved in one particular relationship. For just this reason we seek each other out again. So we can quite naturally assume that a large number of our encounters have so-called "karmic origins".

I emphasise this because in my counselling practice I frequently encounter an approach to this question of karma which I consider to be unhealthy. What typically occurs is the following: two people, a woman and a man, usually with a considerable age gap - he is 40 or 50 and she is 25 or 30 - both of whom had until now been in stable relationships and life-situations, meet and are at once "carried away". It is not only the famous love at first sight, there is something else there : the two people have the experience in their encounter of recognising each other and that this changes everything; from the very first moment one is stirred up, one feels one is in an extraordinary situation which means that one sees the whole of one's life so far, indeed the whole world, differently and, as it were from a distance. Both parties feel that this relationship is the beginning of a whole new life for each of them. Never before have they got on so well with anyone; they seem to be able to communicate almost without words and explanations. And sure enough the observation is made "It must have been our karma to meet".

If we observe how such encounters progress, we can begin to wonder whether we really are dealing with a so-called "karmic" encounter in the sense that the two concerned now need to continue on their path through life together. Typically the two parties quickly decide that they ought to get married. This is required by the close karmic bond that they feel unites them. They overturn all that has gone before, abruptly break off their existing relationships and always use the argument that after all it was karma that brought them together and that is why they have to act in this way.

But often already before they get married, after a few months in any case, we notice a dent in this until now ecstatic relationship, which had started with both feeling they were one and the same person. Suddenly and to the consternation of those concerned there is some kind of disappointment, an awkward feeling, a little failure to understand. And now the whole thing implodes. The blissful state of union turns into an aggressive and desperate tension - desperate because the partners urgently want to get back to the previous state of bliss, but do not know how to do so. Something has broken. They now live through a long and painful crisis before an actually quite normal, very earthly relationship develops which often is dogged for years by the disappointment that the early ecstatic peak of their encounter has gone. Or there is a quick separation. In this case one can safely assume that at least one of the partners, usually the younger one, will soon be involved in another such "karmic" encounter, and again it will be experienced as the ultimate.

What is going on here? If one has the opportunity to accompany the relationship as a counsellor over a longer period of time one frequently finds the following: the older partner in the relationship had come to the point of wondering what their profession, previous marriage or indeed their whole life so far was about. He could feel that there was something in him that had not come to expression in his life thus far - perhaps he had an artistic streak, for example. Now he comes across a younger woman, someone who has perhaps more future than he, and who seems to embody in her life just the things that he seems to be missing. At once this woman becomes the screen onto which his yearnings are projected. She does so in a way that makes him feel that by being together with this woman, just by being in her company, the unfulfilled part of him would come to fulfilment, would be realised. In other words he is under an illusion.

Instead of taking the initiative himself to at least begin to weave the unfulfilled yearning into the life he has lived so far - which despite its one-sidedness does after all belong to him, and which he cannot now simply deny or cancel - or instead of at least finding some way to connect the new with the old, he chooses the apparently simpler way of realising his unfulfilled yearnings by sharing in the life of another person. But that is not how the "I" connects with the Earth. On the contrary, we are dealing here with a kind of partial renunciation of the ego. He delegates the realisation of his own talents to another person. Hence the symbiotic character of such relationships, where the two partners seem to have merged into one.

On the part of the younger woman there is a complementary weakness of the ego in the sense that she has reached a dead-end in the life she has led hitherto and now believes that she can gain security in that her way of life is given added value by the projected yearnings of her partner. She simply perceives that she is living something for which he yearns. And that, she believes, will give her security. What is actually happening is that she is borrowing ego-forces from him. Outwardly it may then appear that she is the leading partner, the one who gives the relationship a direction. In reality she is merely the director of a script which has been written not by her, but by him; a script which until now lay dormant within him and which he now believes he can play out in the relationship with her.

We see, then, that such relationships lack ego-force. What could be "karmic" about a relationship like this? The experience of instant intimacy and immediate understanding is precisely not an indication of karmic links. For, as I have tried to show, each of the partners is under an illusion, a self-delusion.

There is, however, another aspect of this which may well have karmic origins: in the above situation each partner is placing him/herself at the other's disposal, which serves as a screen for the other's projections. The deflation that regularly occurs after a short period demands a considerable willingness to suffer, if one is prepared to endure it. In this willingness to endure suffering for the other and on account of the other, indeed also vis-à-vis one's own delusion, there may be something at work which is the fruit or opportunity arising out of an earlier encounter of the same two individualities.

Whatever the circumstances we should always beware of attributing a karmic background to early experiences of familiarity, of strong sympathy or indeed strong antipathy, even if they are not as dramatic as those described above. I have the impression that such primal feelings on a first encounter may rather be the clothing which memories of a past life take on and which memories may well be triggered by a personality on the basis of some behavioural trait or even some aspect of their appearance. Thus for instance a person A meets a person B who speaks a certain dialect. At once there arise in person A images of a certain landscape and way of life which seem very familiar. It is like a kind of recognition, although person A has in fact not had the opportunity in this life of becoming closely acquainted with this landscape. I consider it quite possible that person A is actually remembering a fragment of a previous life. Typically there is always a mood of yearning around such an experience. It is not simply a memory. For person A it feels as if she/he wants something of or in this landscape but does not know what.

Such processes in the soul are quite different from the karmic encounter of two individualities. In such a situation there may be no karmic relationship at all, or at least very little. It is not the encounter of two egos. On the contrary, if an enduring relationship develops from it one has as an observer the impression that there is a certain one-sidedness and even superficiality in the manner in which person A relates to person B. A limits B in a certain way to the aspect which B called to life in A when they first met. Thus it really is not the encounter of two egos which is after all characterised by the fact that we are also curious about those aspects of the other with which we are not yet familiar and which allows us to experience perhaps contradictory aspects of the other as still being expressions of one and the same individuality. So the experience we have described, whilst by no means as dramatic as the first, is nevertheless similar. In the first case idealised self-images were conjured up by the encounter, and in the second, yearnings which may have resulted from unfulfilled aspects of a previous life. In neither case is there a comprehensive renewed encounter of two individualities but rather it is only parts or extracts of personalities which relate to each other. Generally relationships resulting from these encounters do not have staying power and in my opinion they constitute unsuitable criteria for deciding whether there was indeed a karmic background to them.

Now an apparently similar example which may however lead us closer to the question as to what the real criteria might be for determining a karmic background to an encounter between two people. We are concerned now with a pattern of relationship between a parent and child, a pattern which is very commonly found. There might be, for example, a strongly phlegmatic child and a mainly choleric mother. The older the child becomes, the more difficult the mother finds it to maintain a calm and secure relationship with it. She simply cannot cope with its ponderous ways. She is constantly nagging the child. In the end she drags the child from one doctor or therapist to the next because she fears that the child might be a late developer or even handicapped. Over the years she has to struggle more and more against a systematic revulsion, a systematic antipathy towards this child whose (from her point of view) Buddha-like attitude to the necessities of everyday life at home and at school she not only does not understand but fundamentally rejects. It is also typical of this constellation, which can occur among other polar opposite types as well, that the other parent can cope with the child perfectly well and has no concerns about it.

Here too we are dealing with a projection. Here too the other person is acting as a reflecting surface for the projections of the first.

To begin with the child is driven ever deeper into the one-sidedness of its phlegmatic temperament by the one-sidedness of its mother's approach to it, and seems indeed to confirm the mother's fears and judgements. However, usually around the ninth year, something else makes itself felt in the child. It feels, without being able to articulate the feeling, that it is something other than what the mother sees in it. It begins to try to break through the image that has been attributed to its personality. It might for instance develop enormous ambition in relation to a relatively minor aspect of its life. Perhaps it likes canoeing. Contrary to all other obligations the child takes everything to do with this very seriously, deals with its canoeing equipment very carefully (unlike anything else) etc. The mother interprets this as evidence that her pushing and her bringing up of the child have at least borne some fruit in one area. As an outside observer one can see however, that the child is actually becoming self-reliant and is independently building up an area in its life in which it can be different from how it is perceived. Why canoeing? Well that was the one activity where the mother had not been pushing it, because she did not consider it important.

Similar developments towards a calm well-defined individualisation increase and it can often be several years before the mother recognises how one-sidedly she has viewed her child. Only now is she able to see how her tense battling against the apparent phlegmatic in her child was actually a battle against her own double. She realises with difficulty and embarrassment that she herself had from her early childhood wished to let herself go, to be laid back. Her strict and achievement-oriented parents had denied her this wish, had driven it out of her. Thus phlegmatic traits had acquired a negative slant in her eyes, and she had in fact projected her own shadow onto her child.

Now this situation may seem to be similar to the first one described, in which I do not consider the karmic aspect to be a primary one. But this relationship between a parent and a child does nevertheless have certain characteristics which lead me to the conclusion that there is indeed a considerable karmic background to it and I believe we can even guess at what it might be. Unlike the first example, only one party is projecting onto the other here. Moreover the projection is not there at the outset but rather gradually develops and in the end gets out of control over the course of years. Finally after a long, hard struggle it is recognised as such and withdrawn, with the result that now - the child might be 11, 12 or 13 years old - both parties are left as individuals vis-à-vis themselves and each other who are independent, clearly delineated, multi-layered and autonomous. Only now, after so many years, can one speak of the encounter of egos. Both the mother and the child have worked their way through to this ego-encounter, against inner resistance and with constant effort of their own will. A child like this - and one should take the words literally - has actually served its mother. It served her in the sense that it enabled her to come to terms with her own double and eventually to recognise it as a part of her own personality and thus to attain a comprehensive individualisation. In my opinion a soul would only take on such a task on the basis of a strong karmic bond with the other. Moreover it does not do so casually or perforce but it actually wills it so. Here, I believe, we may conclude that this soul has taken on this act of service to the other as a pre-birth intention arising out of a prior and close spiritual and soul encounter. What leads me to this conclusion is the great doggedness, determination and effort of will with which the pattern of this relationship is seen through and forged into something new.

Karmic encounters are after all not simply there to enable one to reel off or just repeat what has resulted from the relationship with the same individuality in a previous life. Nor are they there to enable a long-held wish or yearning, whether from this life or the last, to be fulfilled. They only have any meaning in that they lead to something new, and that they do so, not in the heady and one might say cheap way illustrated in the first example, but with great and determined effort. In the later example two people had to work their way through to their own "I" and to the "I" of the other. There lies for me the purpose and value of karmic encounter.

Thus we have hit on a feature that we can take as a positive criterion for a karmic background to a relationship: if karma is at work, then the destiny connection will be found in the will. If my will is challenged in the relationship with another then it seems to me that points to an old relationship. That is quite different from spontaneous sympathy or antipathy. It also seems to me to be typical that the working of karma is not revealed but unfolds gradually and with great determination.

Let us take a simple, in a certain sense minor example : one meets a person, perhaps just superficially; the parting of ways follows quite soon. Later on, perhaps as I fall asleep on the same day, thoughts, ideas and plans go through my head and now the question arises: what would the person I met this morning, albeit only briefly, say to these thoughts ? What attitude would this person adopt or how would he react in the same situation I am thinking of ? One seems to want something of this other person or perhaps even to do something with him. Perhaps one is seeking approval, or maybe wishing to come to terms with the person on a deeper level. And as time goes by one is somehow unable to shake off the impression the person has left. One is preoccupied with it. Characteristically the question one is left with is : would this person support me, would this person's will go in the same direction ? I might even find the courage to ask this person's advice.

Consider the subtle but significant difference between this example and the kind of support that was looked for by the younger woman in the first example. In that case there was not involvement of the will; the issue was wish fulfilment and there was never a question of coming to terms but rather of silent understanding, indeed, a fusion of attitudes and aims.

So encounters which affect or awaken the will probably have a strong karmic background. One could imagine that the previous relationship was that of teacher to pupil or parent to child.

One sometimes dreams of such apparently trivial encounters, and then the dream will often have a characteristic gesture: the person in question comes up to one in the dream and addresses one. Or someone emerges from the crowd or from some other confused impression and turns out to be the person in question. In the dream there is often a feeling of expectation: who is this ? What does this person want of me ? Or what do I want of this person ?

The fact that the will is engaged seems to me to be the essential criterion. This leads to another aspect of our topic which in my opinion is too often ignored. Rudolf Steiner repeatedly stated it quite clearly, amongst other places in a lecture given on 27.8.1906 (GA95): "One should not be so concerned with the past aspect of the law of karma as with the future". After all, what is the purpose of karmic encounters? Certainly not the fatalistic reeling off of old patterns. The purpose must be oriented towards the future. When we seek out souls to whom we were once close it is because we have intentions. The question of karma should thus be turned round and directed towards the future. I take up a relationship I have had before so that something new can arise, both for me and for the other. We thus connect with old karma in order to fashion new karma. This can only happen here on Earth. That is the whole reason why we keep coming back. So that we can develop with each other, not so we can simply repeat old patterns of behaviour.

Moreover we also make new relationships with people with whom we may have no karmic bond as yet, or perhaps only a slender one. Here too it is not the mere fact that one knows someone which creates new karma but rather it is when one has something substantial to do with the other. This means that one's will is brought into play by the other person, that one is challenged, when questions are brought into one's life which had never previously occupied one, but which one recognises as fruitful and productive. In such a case it may often be that one is unable in reality to round things off in the relationship. One loses touch, or circumstances prevent one from getting closer or deeper into the relationship. Perhaps even the fact that we share everyday matters means that destiny questions get lost in the mundane routines of life. Just this might mean that I have the urge to seek out the same soul in the next life and to take up the relationship precisely on the basis of the will-impulse that was initiated in this one. Now I see it as my task to bring to Earth what was prepared with this person in the last life.

Let us look once more at the phlegmatic child in the third

example: perhaps it was a ruler by nature, perhaps its life-situation last time meant that it was served. Then it may have occurred to it in an encounter with the soul which this time was its mother to wonder whether its whole potentiality was fulfilled by being waited on, hand and foot. Its situation in life may not have permitted it, perhaps on the grounds of tradition, to step out of this role of being served. Nevertheless deep in its soul the resolve might have arisen out of this encounter to serve another human being's development, not in a superficial way but as a helping hand. With this unfulfilled resolve the soul then passed into the spiritual world and the resolve became one of the motives which led it to seek out the soul concerned, this time in the role of its mother, and having foreknowledge of the fact that she would be one-sided in the way described. So the two work their way through to a mature encounter of egos on the basis of the service performed by the child, there arises something which in my opinion can give rise to yet another form of karmic encounter in the following life, which I have not yet described.

This calm and sure recognition of each other does after all exist. It is quite different from the intoxicated, excited form of encounter initially described which is overlaid with yearning and which is essentially an illusory experience of recognition. Here the recognition is characterised by relaxed sureness. We have here two human beings who recognise each other because they have already gone through a great deal with each other and on account of each other. This unexcited recognition is the fruit of perhaps a whole series of karmic encounters of these two individualities. Those concerned can pick up where they left off quite naturally, but without any turbulent emotions, as if they had parted only the day before. Such encounters in my opinion have the quality of brotherliness. They no longer need the everyday relationship. They might meet from time to time, perhaps only once a year. Yet they are able to exchange thoughts about significant things in such an intimate and fruitful way that one can see they have a common history. This type of relationship does also exist.

If we ask what leads into the future in such a relationship then it might be that a yearning arises in these two individualities to share everyday life again and a yearning might arise deep within them for soul or even physical intimacy. In the next life the two meet again as lovers but lovers whose relationship does not begin with the drama of the first example but whose love gradually develops and endows the relationship with great stability. These are the couples who seem to radiate something, a faithfulness and mutual trust that might seem old-fashioned in some places today. One has the feeling that these two people form a vessel together, in complete freedom and without having to struggle their way through to it, for an angel whose yearning it might have been to be able to pour itself into such a free relationship in order to achieve its tasks. Hence the quality of radiance about such mature relationships. One can see then that there is more at stake than personal karma.

Coleridge : a Life illumined

Coralee Schmandt

In recent years, an astonishing number of new biographies of major poets of the nineteenth century have appeared: of the Romantic poets, Keats, Shelley, and Coleridge; of the American Transcendentalist, Ralph Waldo Emerson, as well as of the visionary poet, William Blake[1]. Although these poets cannot be categorised neatly under one rubric, all can be said to be part of one "movement", one upsurging of creative energy, one flood of inspiration for humanity that arose in England during the volatile time around the French Revolution, and ultimately played itself out in America through Emerson, Thoreau, Dickinson, and Whitman.

We might ask ourselves why just at this time these poets' lives and poetry are being re-evaluated. What has prompted this outpouring of interest in the lives and works of these representatives of the Spirit of our Time? Do they perhaps have a message for us in our time? Are we being given an opportunity to hear something particularly relevant to us now as we face the enormous challenges confronting us? For all these poets champion nature and the human soul, the imagination, and the individual inner activity that not only can save us from soul death, but also is the first step toward unfolding consciously latent higher capacities within us.

We might also wonder what can be said that is new about these poets that one cannot find in existing biographies? In fact, the difference between earlier biographies and modern ones lies not so much in the biographical data as in a new sensibility or consciousness that pervades these re-interpretations. Readers today have clearly changed and the biographers are responding to the need of a new generation with new capacities for grasping both the spiritual content of the poets and the complexity of their lives. Let us turn our attention to one modern biographer in particular, Richard Holmes , who has written biographies of Shelley and Coleridge, and who also appears to have a capacity for meeting these poets and presenting them in a way that opens up at once the man, his life, and the eternal message of the work to the readership. We will focus on his two-volume life of Samuel Taylor Coleridge, *Early Visions* and *Darker Reflections*, first looking at the biographer's approach and then examining the content to see why Coleridge is vitally relevant to us today. Finally, we will explore possibilities for the future of biographies of the poets.

Richard Holmes and Romantic Biography

Called "the most romantic of contemporary biographers and probably the most revolutionary in spirit and form" by his fellow-biographer, Michael Holroyd, Holmes is also the most articulate about the new trend in biography that he is helping initiate. In his autobiographical account of his vocation, *Footsteps*[2], he reveals the quality of interest in the Other that has become the driving impulse of his work. Holmes' follows his subject quite literally, actually traversing the landscapes, entering the houses if possible, where these poets lived out their "brief Drama in the Flesh." (E. Dickinson) As well as other influences, Holmes takes into account the formative effect of landscape and atmosphere on the romantic poet's sensibility, realising that, as Coleridge writes, "One of the most noticeable and fruitful facts in psychology is the modification of the same feeling by difference of form. The

Heaven lifts up my soul , the sight of the ocean seems to widen it..." (Coleridge, *Anima Poetae*) Holmes takes such observations seriously; he notes in a footnote that "Coleridge's passion for climbing hills and scaling mountain peaks...seems to have some deep imaginative correspondence with his metaphysical inquiries. The panoramic view from a peak ... often brings moments of intense vision."[3] Richard Holmes understands that life is a journey through an inner as well as an outer landscape and that the latter gives us a symbolic language for experiences of the soul. Therefore, he complements the rigours of his scholarship with actual experience of the backdrops against which his players have enacted their earthly lives.

At the same time as Holmes can enter experientially into the biography of his subject, he also demonstrates objectivity and tolerance; for example, Coleridge's opium addiction or Shelley's tragic amours are treated honestly and non-judgementally, indicating that both the biographer's and our boundaries of understanding have evidently expanded and that we have perhaps learned something of acceptance and compassion through the hard experiences of this century. Holmes does not flinch from describing the most unpleasant physical symptoms of Coleridge's opium addiction, but is able to weave these details into the fabric of his life and higher striving. As a result, we become aware that a judgmental attitude is petty in the face of the richness of life itself. We achieve a kind of spiritual perspective from which we can appreciate that our struggles on the physical plane are part of a larger picture of spiritual development.

Furthermore, in his mission statement , Holmes implicitly acknowledges that the details of a great person's life of personality and destiny ultimately serve "the work", the artistic substance that is generated as the artist pursues his inner quest passionately through life, examines it with intensity and immediacy in journals, letters and lectures, and concentrates and potentises it in poetry. "I believe passionately that one of the main purposes of a literary life is to renew the appreciation of-no, the love of-a neglected literary work, and to make it alive for a new generation."[4] But the door to the work can be opened through a sympathetic relationship with the bearer of the message and this has become the role of biography.

It is enlightening, in connection with these observations, to look at what Rudolf Steiner has said regarding present and future human capacities. In *The Work of the Angels in Man's Astral Body*, as well as in other lectures, Steiner describes new impulses that human beings will receive from their angels, "...Out of the spiritual world men will receive an impulse through their Angel that will kindle a far deeper interest in every human being...By a sudden impetus a certain secret will be inspired into man from the spiritual side namely, *what the other man really is*." (p.14) When Holmes applies himself with such loving interest to his subject, immersing himself in the words and deeds of another person through years of study, he arrives at an experience of "what the other man really is." He finds himself in what he calls an "imaginary relationship", a "relationship of trust" between himself and his subject. He comes to recognise the "integrity" of character, "the moral continuity between the inner and outer man"; in other words, he has intimations of the questing human spirit that soars beyond the exigencies of the earthly destiny and of the individual mind's path of inquiry or the karmic question which impels the life. "There is between (the biographer and his subject) a ceaseless discussion , a reviewing and questioning of motives and actions and consequences,.... It is fictional, imaginary, because of course the subject cannot really, literally, talk back; but the biographer must come to act and think of his subject as if he can."[5]

As a result of this deepened imagination of his subject, a new picture of the poet's personality emerges for him and the subject can actually begin to work on the biographer. For example, having followed Shelley on his restless wandering through Italy, Holmes is stirred to new idealism himself. "I left my balcony at San Terenzo early one crisp November morning, determined to bring the angel to earth , and to do justice to Shelley's lifelong dream of a better world here below."[6]

Nowadays we are looking for living ideals that can work into our daily lives. Shelley's real significance for us has been damaged by the effete image of him that was perpetrated after his death and which contrasts strikingly with the robust, impassioned character of unshakeable ideals Holmes brings to life in his biography, *The Pursuit*. Likewise, Coleridge lost credibility by being cast as the sedentary "sage of Highgate" but through Holmes' two-volume biography we meet and are inspired by the passionate young Coleridge who regularly strode the 20 miles over Dunmail Pass between Keswick and Grasmere in all weathers, notebooks in hand, in his ardour to see the Wordsworths, as well as by the charismatic lecturer and conversationalist who could hold his audiences rapt through the power of his presence and brilliant intuitive thought. The result of "romanticising" or actually sentimentalising these poets in the past has rendered them less effectual because they have been perceived as "otherworldly" and therefore out of touch with our daily reality. "Bringing the angel to earth" means at once humanising him and elevating him to his stature as an inspiring individual with a significant message for us today. Then these poets can remind us that living words can change the world and that lives that over-brim with enthusiasm for the spirit can inspire and lead humanity forward in the age of the consciousness soul.

Coleridge's Path

In fact, Richard Holmes' approach to biography emulates just those characteristics of Coleridge that he describes when he says Coleridge "actively hunts down the otherness of being." As Coleridge himself so vividly puts it, "It is easy to cloathe Imaginary Beings with our own Thoughts & Feelings; but to send ourselves out of ourselves, to *think* ourselves in to the Thoughts and Feelings of Beings in circumstances wholly & strangely different from our own: hoc labor, hoc opus: and who has achieved it ? Perhaps only Shakespeare."[7] Coleridge recognised that Shakespeare's power to become one with other forms of being, be it cloud, or rose, or characters in his plays together with "his endless activity of thought" were primary elements of imagination, of poetic power. Coleridge himself cultivated these higher imaginative faculties through an active self-training in observation of the nuances of growth and change in the natural world. For, as Coleridge knew, we have latent capacities that can be developed if we apply ourselves. "In short, all the organs of Sense are framed for a corresponding World of Sense; and we have it. All the organs of Spirit are framed for a corresponding World of Spirit: & we cannot but believe it. The Infidel proves only that the latter organs are not yet developed in him."[8] Those familiar with Steiner's exercises for developing higher consciousness will recognise correspondences with his exercises for developing imagination through plant or cloud observation. As Holmes emphasises in this regard, Coleridge was a most extraordinary observer of nature for what it could reveal of the workings of the divine in our world and for the metaphors that could actualise his insights into the nature of the human soul. He was particularly attentive to shifts of light, the movement of clouds, the play of water, observations which he seized upon imaginatively in the moment of apprehension and jotted quickly into his notebook in vividly alive, almost panting "shorthand". For example, "River Greta near its fall into the Tees - Shootings of water threads down the slope of the huge green stone - the white

Eddy-rose that blossom'd up against the stream in the scallop, by fits & starts, obstinate in resurrection -- It is the life that we live...."[9] Here Coleridge exhibits the attention to detail of a scientist, the interest of a nature enthusiast, and the wonder of the poet and the child. Elsewhere he describes a poet's capacities: " for all sounds & forms of human nature he must have the *ear* of a wild Arab listening in the silent Desert - the *eye* of a North American Indian tracing the footsteps of an Enemy upon the Leaves that strew the Forest: the *Touch* of a Blind Man feeling the face of a darling Child."[10] Filled with child-like reverence, Coleridge was uniquely attuned to metamorphic changes where as one form passes over into another the spiritual can be perceived working in the processes of Nature as an invisible formative power within all manifest forms. "Starlings in vast flights drove along like smoke, mist, or any thing misty without volition - now a circular area inclined in an Arc - now a Globe - now from complete Orb into an Ellipse & Oblong - now a balloon with the car suspended, now a concaved Semicircle -- & still it expands and condenses, some moments glimmering & shivering, dim & shadowy, now thickening, deepening, blackening."[11] Accurate observation was always a stimulus to imaginative thinking for him.

Such self-initiated exercises in perception, born of love for nature and the spirit, revealed to Coleridge the creative spirit of the universe weaving in the vital activity of the world and in the creative mind of man, the divine Word that speaks through the created universe. Speaking to his infant son in "Frost at Midnight", he foresees the future of his "Child of Nature" who will grow up reading that divine script:

> ....so shalt thou see and hear
> The lovely shapes and sounds intelligible
> Of that eternal language, which thy God
> Utters, who from eternity doth teach

Himself in all, and all things in himself...

What he has apprehended imaginatively in his poem above, he later interprets thus in his *Religious Musings:* "For all that meets the bodily sense I deem Symbolical, one mighty alphabet", expressing philosophically what he had earlier uttered poetically.

As one follows the course of Coleridge's life in Holmes' biography, one can actually participate in Coleridge's creative process as his nature observation re-emerges transformed into poetic imagery. The "Eddy-rose...obstinate in resurrection" that struck him as an image of Life itself offers another example of how perception becomes poetry and later philosophy in the life of thought of Coleridge. We find that the central images of both "The Rime of the Ancient Mariner" and "Dejection: An Ode" evoke this picture of "the Life we live" from his journal. In the first, The Ancient Mariner, "alone on the wide, wide sea", abandoned by God and by Nature, burdened by his guilt and surrounded by death, comes to a point of utter bleakness and despair. Yet, even then, stirred by beauty , by the colours and movement of the water-snakes, he can find the power in his heart to bless and it arises in him like the Eddy-rose at the foot of the waterfall. Thereby he releases himself and Nature from the evil he as the representative human being has perpetrated in the world.

A spring of love gushed from my heart
And I blessed them unaware....

Later in "Dejection: An Ode", the same inner "fountain", which is "Joy", is that spiritual power within that can renew not only our perception of Nature but Nature herself.

"Joy, Lady! Is the spirit and the power,
Which wedding Nature to us gives in dower
A new Earth and new Heaven,...."

Not only can our own souls find life through such capacities in the human heart amid the desolation of modern consciousness, but Nature too is dependent on the discovery by human beings of the fount within, their own inner powers of resurrection.

"O Lady! We receive but what we give
And in our life alone does Nature live:..."

That is to say, we must now actively "give", i.e., initiate engagement with the world around us not only to keep our own souls alive but also the Soul of the World.

As Coleridge passes into the later phases of his life we can trace a path from participatory perception through imaginative thinking to apprehension of the spirit. Through the struggles and pain of his arduous life, he came to recognise that the heart's infinite powers of resurrection in the midst of desolation and despair are "the healing powers of Christ."[12] Further, in the *Biographia Literaria,* he defined the creative power of the poet, Imagination, a "a repetition in the finite mind of the eternal act of creation in the infinite I AM." Rising into metaphysical heights, he transcends Reason or thinking and achieves direct spiritual insight or the realm of "Religion".

"...Religion passes out of the ken of Reason only where the eye of Reason has reached its own Horizon; and that Faith is then but its continuation: even as the Day softens away into the sweet Twilight, and Twilight, hushed and breathless, steals into the Darkness. It is Night, sacred Night! The upraised Eye views only the starry Heaven... and the outward Beholding is fixed on the sparks twinkling in the aweful depth... only to preserve the Soul steady and collected in its pure *Act* of inward Adoration to the great I AM, and to the filial WORD that re-affirmeth it from Eternity to Eternity, whose choral Echo is the Universe."[13]

So we see how Coleridge forged a path from beauty to truth , from the imaginative perception of nature to the reality of the spirit through his own alert and questioning heart-thinking. "I teach a real existence of a Spiritual World without a material."[14] Holmes' biography inspires us to recognise in Samuel Taylor

Coleridge the archetype of the self-initiating seeker fired by the inner power of active imagination that can inspire and give direction to the modern consciousness soul individual. Then Coleridge's words seem to leap the gap between his time and ours as if it were for us he had lived and written. If indeed the times have called forth such biographies that speak so resonantly to us, confirming the spiritual dimension of the human quest, we can imagine that spiritual forces can pour into our time through such conduits, helping to break the spell that has a stranglehold on our feelings, thinking and will, freeing us to become the active co-creators it is our destiny to become. The lives and works of Coleridge and these other poets burn with the fire of enthusiasm for the Imagination united with highest idealism and spiritual seeking. Such biographies can open up to us sources of inspiration when with honesty and open-mindedness, the biographers let their light shine, a beacon for our time.

The Future and Biography

At the end of his entry on Biography in the *Oxford Companion to English Literature,* Richard Holmes refers to the last forty years as the "Golden Age" of biography, but is uncertain about its future. Will it become outmoded with the "increase in electronically available historical databases"? But he concludes,"...it is possible that the English form, which combines so wonderfully the imaginative and the critical spirit, has triumphs yet to come."[15]

I suggest that biography may even evolve new forms as humanity begins to awaken to questions of destiny and the spiritual tasks of individuals and groups of individuals who share a common task. For example, will we one day have the capacity to penetrate with insight the significance of those earthly "meetings" between Coleridge and his contemporaries: Keats, Emerson, Wordsworth, as well as the possible meetings that never took place on the earthly plane, such as between Coleridge and Shelley or Blake ? And what of the kinship with precursors who kindled the poetic spirit in the poets of a later generation and inspired the recognition of their own tasks in the unfolding spiritual life of humankind? Will we one day get beyond talking of "influences" and develop "biographies" that trace the spiritual kinship of Coleridge to Shakespeare, for example, or Shakespeare to Spenser or Chaucer? Furthermore, could karmic research one day unfold for us the significance of Italy, for example, for Coleridge, Shelley, Keats, and Emerson, for whom Italy in different ways represented life and health and inspiration as Steiner describes it did for Goethe? "Goethe could not live without having seen Rome and a culture which, however antiquated, still enshrined the spiritual in the sensory-physical..[16] And finally, in the "web of lives" that weaves between individuals brought together for some greater cultural end, can we foresee a time when we could recognise what forces of world destiny are at work? Holmes hints at such a possibility when, in one astounding flash of insight, he perceives a connection between the bonfire on the island in Grasmere Lake that inaugurates the Romantic movement when Wordsworth and Coleridge and their families danced joyfully around the fire, and the bonfire on the beach at Lerici twenty-one years later which consumed the drowned body of Percy Shelley, also marking the end of the most poetically productive years of Wordsworth, Coleridge, Shelley, of course, and Keats who had died in Rome the year before.[17] Here symbolically we catch a glimpse of the interconnectedness of all these individuals in the one great surge we call the Romantic movement, that embraced other poets, artists, and thinkers in other countries in one in-pouring of spiritual insight. These poets represent a powerful spiritual impulse, a last evocation of the old imaginative consciousness and a vision for the future, that is re-entering present-day culture through renewed interest in their lives and work. Woven together by invisible threads, this network of individuals was fulfilling a common purpose of significance for human development. Perhaps not one of them was conscious of the role they shared in common, but together they focused the beams of heavenly insight into a kindling ray that can light our way into a future they foresaw for us.

References

1 Motion, Andrew *Keats,* Faber and Faber, 1997; Richardson, Robert, *Emerson, The Mind on Fire,* University of California Press, 1995; Ackroyd, Peter, *Blake,* Sinclair-Stevenson 1995; Holmes, Richard, *Shelley: The Pursuit,* Harper Collins 1974; Holmes, Richard, *Coleridge: Early Visions,* Penguin, 1989; and Holmes, Richard, *Coleridge: Darker Reflections,* Harper Collins, 1998

2 Holmes, Richard *Footsteps: Adventures of a Romantic Biographer,* Vintage Books, 1985

3 Holmes, Richard *Early Visions,* p.324

4 Holmes, Richard *Darker Reflections,* p.563

5 Holmes, Richard *Footsteps,* p.66

6 ibid., p.198

7 Holmes, Richard *Early Visions,* Penguin 1990 p.326

8 Holmes, Richard *Darker Reflections,* p.253

9 Holmes, Richard *Early Visions,* p.247

10 ibid., p.326

11 ibid., p.253-4

12 Holmes, Richard *Darker Reflections,* p.359

13 ibid., p.412

14 ibid., p.460

15 *The Oxford Companion to English Literature,* OUP 1998 ed. M. Drabble, see *Biography*

16 Steiner, Rudolf *The Arts and Their Mission,* Anthroposophic Press 1964 p.54

17 Holmes, Richard *Early Visions* p.277

A Biographical Fragment

Nick Thomas

I was four years old I think (I was born in 1941) when I asked my mother to show me how to do magic, which she promised to do when I was a little older. When I reminded her a year or two later she started showing me how to do conjuring tricks. I immediately reacted by saying that was not what I meant! At that early age I was somehow well aware of the difference between magic and conjuring.

When I was nine I thought much about immortality, and I remember feeling more than daunted by the idea of existing "for ever and ever and ever". However I was convinced it had to be faced as it was inconceivable to me that my thinking-centre would vanish at death.

In my late teens I became interested in occult matters through the novels of Dennis Wheatley. In particular the book *Strange Conflict* rang loud bells in me, for the descriptions of astral travelling and related matters seemed to be much more than mere fiction. I started reading everything I could in the library on psychic research and then Theosophy. This revived my earlier request to my mother about magic, and I became intent on performing levitation and geared myself up to learn its secret in a dream. I did indeed wake up in the middle of the night with a solution, which was so obvious that I did not bother to write it down on the carefully placed piece of paper available for the purpose. Alas, in the morning it was beyond the reach of my memory! When I was in the Sixth Form, I embarked upon a study of Blavatsky's *Secret Doctrine* which I had to read in the public library in York, where we were living at the time, as it was not for lending out. I diligently made a dictionary of the Sanskrit words she used, but about a third of the way through I found the conflict with Christianity too great. I had become deeply attached to Christ, though not in a Church sense, especially at boarding school where the Gospels were my main comfort and solace. So I abandoned the *Secret Doctrine*, but with a lingering conviction that there was something in it even so. I then saw in a bookshop a copy of the *Grimoire of Solomon* containing many magical formulae and spells. I wrestled with my Christian conscience over this book for weeks, and even copied out and tried one of the formulae in the process, but finally I decided not to buy it. Within a few days I found *Knowledge of Higher Worlds and its Attainment* in the public library. Somehow I had ignored this book for ages, and later when I tried to recollect why, I think I assumed that it would only be a list of books. This was typical of me: I didn't want someone else's list! Anyway, no sooner had I finally opened it than I rushed home with it, hid it away from my parents, and avidly started reading. I only got one third of the way through. The reason was quite different this time: there was so much to do practising the early meditations, and some of the later ones were so obviously beyond me, that it was a long time before I ventured further. Of course I decided to buy the book, and I remember going in my school uniform to collect it from the bookshop where I had ordered it, and being told by the assistant that it was not Christian. I remonstrated hotly and left. For me it combined Christianity and all that I had a lingering respect for in Blavatsky, even though no direct mention is made of Christ.

Two years later, by which time I was undergoing an engineering training in the RAF, my mother gave me as a present the little book *Flying Saucers: Physical and Spiritual*

Aspects by Georg Unger. She knew my interest in this subject at that time. The importance for me lay not in the content but in the list of books by Steiner on the flyleaf! I sent away for these as fast as I could read them and soon built up quite a library. I have often wondered what the RAF sergeant who daily inspected the cleanliness of my room made of such titles as *The Spiritual Beings in the Heavenly Bodies!* Eventually when I had read a great deal it dawned on me that there must be a society of some kind where I could meet other people interested in these things, for I was very lonely spiritually. So I ventured down to London one Saturday in my second year at College intent upon finding out what was going on in Bloomsbury Square (the address in my copy of the *Knowledge of Higher Worlds and its Attainment*). Alas there was nothing there any more, so on another Saturday I thought it might be worth asking the publishers, and went to 35 Park Road. There to my amazement was none other than Rudolf Steiner House! I met Roma Browne who was the then Secretary of the AS in GB, and who became a lifelong friend thereafter. I also met Lisa Palmer in the Library. By then I had decided to join the Roman Catholic Church, as after my brush with *The Secret Doctrine* I felt the church I belonged to was weak and shallow, and the sterner stuff of the Catholics was necessary as Christianity was important above all. In view of this I more or less had to bully Lisa into sponsoring me to join the Society, whereas Roma recognised where I was spiritually and readily agreed.

My becoming a Roman Catholic partly enabled my mother to return to that faith, which she had left on marriage. Another consequence was that my brother also became a Catholic. I suspect one reason why I joined was to free her to do so, as fairly soon after I refused confirmation because Anthroposophy waxed ever stronger in me, and eventually after a row with my mother I left the RC Church. My experience of spiritual freedom on doing so was unexpectedly strong, for I retain a genuine respect for it to this day. In deciding to go against my mother, which was not easy as we were always very close, I stood firmly on the ground given me by *The Philosophy of Spiritual Activity*. This was a big crisis in my life, and that book was my mainstay.

I was very shocked at school when the colour of an object was explained as that part of the light which was reflected by it. For some reason I rejected this idea completely, and increasingly I felt a gulf between what I felt about things and the way they were explained scientifically. Often I was irritated by the fact that explanations were given and then later shown to be mere approximations, for example the idea of a perfectly smooth body was assumed and then later it was explained no such 'beast' exists. More irritation when no perfectly black body could exist. I seemed to wish these idealisations to have their place in reality. Such experiences led me not to go along with all that was being taught as fast as I otherwise might, which extended all the way to my later engineering training, but on the other hand I was intensely interested in physics, and spent most of my boring French lessons trying to invent anti-gravity. As my father was a doctor in the RAF we frequently moved, and the casualties resulting from the disruption in schooling were French, piano playing and maths. Latin never even came in sight! I tended to get 32% in maths, but in the middle of a geometry exam just two terms before O-level I suddenly saw what I was supposed to do. No-one had ever explained, or more likely I had never grasped, that theorems were supposed to be used to prove other things, and that a question expected the use of this procedure for its solution! Anyway, helped by this blinding revelation half way through that exam, I beavered away feverishly and got 50%. My maths master said in a subsequent report that my progress amazed him. I then went on to take A-level exams, which previously had seemed quite beyond consideration. All this adds up to a feature of my whole biography: the constant feeling that difficult practical things as well as clever academic things were beyond me. Life kept showing me otherwise, often in the kindest way.

My decision to study electrical engineering sprang from an interest I had in logic and its application to computer circuits. I was not good enough for an academic career anyway, and my father encouraged me to join the RAF and be trained there. It was an excellent training, and my typically slow and late academic waking-up process continued after that, so that by the time I left I was told I would be sent to university after a spell of duty in the field. This never happened, but it illustrates this continuing thread through my life, and was later confirmed when I was one of the few to gain an A1 pass in postgraduate study at the RAF College. Engineering was just right for me as it was the polar opposite of my idealistic approach, constantly balancing it by hard necessities. Real systems are never perfect and much more time is spent in dealing with all the imperfections than on aesthetically pleasing general ideas and principles. Even so I constantly veered towards the latter, and even proposed a research project to produce an ideal control system. I learnt a great deal from finding out just why it would not work.

I had varied experiences in the RAF, working on aircraft maintenance, flight simulators, radar, computers and long-range communications. I endlessly asked to be posted to a research job, but was never granted that. I left the RAF in 1979 and had a sabbatical, following the work of Lawrence Edwards, and I met and became a friend of John Wilkes, developing an interest in his flowforms and problems connected with water. After a few years I took a job with the Canadian company

Northern Telecom (now Nortel) working on data communication. Then in 1975 I was asked to become General Secretary of the AS in GB.

My interest in physics and science remained throughout all this, and was further stimulated by my study of Steiner's ideas, and from my early twenties I sought for a satisfactory way of relating Steiner's research to mainstream discoveries and knowledge. Eventually I came to study projective geometry and, stimulated by a comment by Olive Whicher about the lemniscate, sought a genuinely projective construction for it. While in Turkey with plenty of time I finally thought I had found this along with other things, and Lawrence Edwards alone answered my letters about it in a most helpful way. This led me to a knowledge of the work of George Adams, and an interest in the idea of a negative, or counter-space. All along, my engineer's approach demanded a detailed way of understanding how the etheric body actually relates to the physical, and projective geometry seemed the best approach. What I meant then by this question was: what is different in the activity of the physical body due to the presence of the etheric body, and how does that work? Are subtle heat balances different from those we would expect physically, or is space curved in some strange way? Just <u>what</u> is different? This contrasts with general statements such as saying the body grows or takes in nourishment, all of which are obvious but do not explain anything about that connection.

The advent of chaos theory was of great interest to me in all this as it broke the tyranny of the mechanistic explanation of all things. It is genuinely possible to have well defined mechanical systems whose future behaviour cannot be predicted even in principle. It opened the way, to my mind, for complex systems such as living bodies to obey the laws of physics and chemistry and yet also obey other laws.

After 33 years pondering on these things in all sorts of ways I finally had an idea! If an object or entity is in both ordinary and counter space at the same time how will it behave as it tries to obey their very different laws simultaneously? This turned out to be a more far-reaching question than I expected, and the first fruit of it was a new explanation for gravitation. Encouraged by this I followed up the developing notion that there is a threefold situation involving space, counter space and the stress of the beings living in and relating these two. It led to new ways of thinking about liquids, gases, light, chemistry and life, in other words about the elements and ethers. I felt that a science serving Michael should not only be spiritual but also able to account for conventional findings, so that they may be re-thought and understood on a different basis. Also some of the more surprising findings of Steiner himself in relation to science could be understood. Once again, I found myself struggling at the limits of my ability to use the maths needed for some of it. The project is still on the boil and far from complete, since it is a huge one. I was encouraged to write a book about it, but I did not know who to write it for! For specialists? But most of them would not read it. Who anyway would publish it? For general readers? But it seemed important first to establish the ideas as exactly as I was able before giving a more general account that would remain woolly without the existence of a more rigorous exposition. The encouragement of many friends and that of the Science Section in Dornach finally spurred me on. Writing a book: something else that I had never really thought I would do!

One aspect of biography became clear to me through all this: I had in the course of my life followed up many interests and struggled with academic books well beyond my initial expertise. I fought to understand Einstein, quantum physics and the like, and waded through dense mathematical texts checking every (often poorly explained) step. The balance struck in such books between boring over-explanation and elegant economical exposition was not often on my side. All these threads of interest converged in the work described above, and the reasons for these often seemingly disparate interests found their place. Thus the reasons for our varied interests can eventually become clear and find a context.

I cannot imagine life without anthroposophy, without a Christian notion of reincarnation and karma, without other anthroposophists. Yet I have sensed on some occasions that there were other paths I could have taken in life as real possibilities, not just theoretical ones. Karma is not a "tramline" affair, but weaves together several life-paths as real possibilities, leaving it to our freedom which to tread. It seems to me more like a colourfully woven fabric of possibilities than a single thread.

Childhood Illnesses: Spiritual Births

Bob Dudney

Similar to the way a person's life unfolds in a series of births every seven years, acute, febrile illnesses are also birth-like processes. And as the first few seven-year births of a human life are the most pronounced (physically and mentally), fevers also tend to be most dramatic in childhood. Before germs came to dominate medical minds, physicians recognized several fevers as uniquely childhood illnesses that used to be common features of a child's life. Medical evidence confirms the anthroposophical appreciation of fevers (including those belonging to childhood) as beneficial to a person's overall, life-long health.

A fever gave birth to Jacques Lusseyran's initiative to form a resistance movement in Nazi-occupied France at age fifteen. His vivid account provides an archetypal picture:

"A bad case of measles declared itself in a few hours and broke out in a rash after four or five days. When it left me, it set a torrent of energy free...In the first few hours of fever it became obvious that my system was purging itself of a poison and spewing out foreign bodies. But the poison was moral as much as it was physical, of that I am sure...This was no microbe or virus making its way in - it was resolve.

"It took me over from head to foot like a conquered land...It was driving me to definite destinations which I had not thought about before it came...

"What a fortunate case of measles that was! In me it had

catalyzed a pack of fears and desires, intentions and irritations which had held me closed in a tight fist for weeks, and which I should never have been able to break open myself. On the first day of convalescence I said to myself aloud in my room: "The Occupation is my sickness."

While every fever does not result in a resistance movement, acute illness can be a turning point, at least to some degree (if one allows it). During a workshop on this theme, a woman shared how a time came in sixth grade when all the adults around her began to be concerned that she was overly worried. Her parents and teachers felt her worried state continuing to increase for about a year and began to say something needed to be done about it. Then she came down with scarlet fever with several days of moderate to high fever and a strong rash. When she recovered, to everyone's relief: her worried state was gone.

Such an experience is characteristic of puberty, when the astral forces are developing a more intensive relationship with bodily processes. In this girl's case, the storm clouds of astral activity gathered over the course of a year, weighing on her life, worrying her. Through a more intensive engagement of the spiritual, ego forces active in the warmth processes of fever, she was able to dissolve and dispel her burden. One can easily surmise she became more able to engage in life after this illness. Hippocrates' statement: "Fever is the flame that cleanses the body" can be understood to include the astral.

Instances of children being transformed after a fever are commonly observed by adults around them. Typical words used to describe the changes are: lighter, more awake, happier, more at ease, more confident, more balanced. New capacities become evident; especially in pre-school children, the next developmental step may be easily taken as the child recovers.

With all birth processes something is being cast off, dying

to make way for the new. In the common cold, for instance, there is discharge of old cells and inflammatory material from the nose. If the illness is more severe, pus-like material indicates a stronger process of death and cleansing. Childhood illnesses frequently involve multiple organs in the renewal process; much of the skin may slough off through a rash.

The heightened metabolic activity of fever lifts one in the polarity of cosmic and earthly. The more cosmic state brings greater possibilities and renewal to the more earthly parts of us. Hence Rudolf Steiner's assertion that childhood illnesses help the child burn up and discard burdensome hereditary influences received from the parents. Fever is basically a strong effort to re-connect with the more heavenly aspects of our being.

Contemporary thinking ignores the considerable evidence febrile illnesses are beneficial and simply reacts to the unpleasant aspects, believing any measure that brings relief must be good. Hence the continued popularity of antibiotics, anti-fever, anti-inflammatory, and analgesic/anti-pain drugs despite ample evidence they generally do more harm than good.

The documented benefits of febrile illnesses include a number of studies that found an inverse relationship between acute and chronic diseases. The fewer fevers (including childhood illnesses) one has, the greater the chances of developing chronic problems such as cancer and multiple sclerosis. Similarly, there is a definite correlation between learning difficulties and antibiotic use for self-limited illnesses like otitis media (erroneously referred to as ear "infection").

It is unique to the human being to have repeated episodes of acute, self-limited illness throughout one's lifetime, in stark contrast to animals. Even domestic animals seldom fully recover from fevers, and are quite likely to succumb entirely, as is the rule in the wild. Only human beings have been blessed with such healing ability, which is intimately related to the uniquely human capacities to learn, to grow, to transform, to discover. Just as cancer relates to diminished capacity for renewal through fever, suppressing the body's inflammatory response with antibiotics tends to diminish one's ability to become, to grow, to learn.

As with anything worthwhile, there is some risk in even the most benign febrile illnesses. One is much more likely, however, to be permanently harmed or die from a motor vehicle accident, yet few would dream of denying themselves such means of travel. Truly rational approaches to managing fevers require appreciation of their benefits, lest the cure be worse than the disease.

Humanity seems to have to learn ever again in yet another way that life is Life: precious, sensitive, cosmic, eternal. We need fever to help us become like Lusseyran: inflamed, enthusiastic, involved - in love.

Verifying Karma Research

Arne Enge, Arne Smit, Stein Schage
Translated from Norwegian by William Forward

In News Sheet No.84 of the Norwegian Anthroposophical Newsletter Jostein Saether writes two articles "A meditative life in relation to one's destiny questions" and "Why I have published my previous incarnations". We should like to make a few comments on the content of these two articles and also to deal with the manner in which they are presented. Saether tries to show how he has worked with Rudolf Steiner's karma exercises and he writes about the results this work has produced. Apart from this the articles consist to a large extent of material from Rudolf Steiner's writings or lectures, supplemented by Saether's personal comments and experiences. In the first article he writes about inner experiences which he maintains give information about his own previous incarnations, whilst in the second he seems to provide an explanation and a defence of his own practice. In doing this he maintains on the one hand that he is working in accordance with the principles of anthroposophy whilst on the other he is "fully conscious of the fact that he breaches the *previously very necessary occult modesty which was the characteristic of all Rudolf Steiner's work*".

Development within culture generally and in the case of individual human beings depends on the courage and ability to depart from what has gone before. No one can say for sure in advance what is right and what is wrong in such matters, nor can one predict what will prove fruitful in the future. Whoever maintains that the truth is something that is given once and for all has already lost it. This is particularly so in the case of anthroposophical work and we must welcome any attempt to further develop either ideas or practice. This is the attitude we wish to bring to Jostein Sæther's work, but we do have very considerable reservations about the content of his articles.

[A section discussing Saether's way of dealing with the source material that he has found in the work of Rudolf Steiner is omitted here.]

On Good and Quick Results - The Key Issue of Time

When one adapts a particular method to work towards a specific goal, the results one expects will of course determine what evidence one selects. Saether writes: "Astonishingly good results have come through". Earlier on he writes "...one can reckon on quick results". Saether is here very much in line with strong tendencies of our age but anyone who is familiar with Steiner's karma exercises will know that these are justified primarily by moral criteria and not by any awareness of "quick results" whether they be Sæther's or anyone else's. Steiner consistently warns against short cuts in this area. In the same lecture to which Saether has referred with regard to the karma exercises, Rudolf Steiner repeatedly mentions the importance of being able to wait when dealing with this type of experience. He points out how he himself had to wait 21 years after the spiritual experience he had in connection with Goethe's fairy tale before he was able to express it in a different form in the first mystery drama. In this context Saether's method, as represented here and in various lectures in Oslo, may appear rather "fresh" and lacking in thoroughness. In the same lecture Rudolf Steiner goes on to say of the experiences one may have in the course of three days when working with this exercise. "If one begins to speak of the experiences to other people, they cease at once. They really must take their course in peace and tranquillity. It is best if no one is aware of such experiences other than the person who has them."

Human development requires time but changes can take place at various speeds in the different layers of the personality. An intellectual achievement may take place quicker than changes in one's feeling life. New inner pictures can arise in one's consciousness without one necessarily being able at once to interpret them - something Saether also emphasises. It may also be that the moral qualities are not yet present to enable one to integrate these new inner experiences into a healthy self-knowledge or into responsible actions towards others.

The Critical Faculty

We are also perturbed by the following remark: "One can of course have one's doubts about what others have experienced in the spirit but in the case of one's own experiences one will be able to find a path through fear and doubt and acquire certainty in respect of identification and spiritual continuity". We believe everyone today is on a slippery slope the moment one loses doubt and the capacity to subject one's inner experiences to critical evaluation. It may mean that Sæther's method contains within itself the need of an uncritical approach when he says: "...I tried during the meditation to concentrate the force of my ego in the direction of my own birth and conception. I pushed my way back, so to speak...." Yet despite the fact that he protests his humility and says that imaginations are always a matter of grace, it seems that here too he has got into an inner dynamic that has precisely the opposite qualities.

Freedom For The "Karma Researcher" - And For Fellow Human Beings

In his article entitled "Why I publish my previous incarnations" Saether makes two important claims. Firstly that he is entitled to pass on details about the karma of other contemporaries where he has judged that the situation is right for such *radical intimacy* Later on he says on the basis of a certain understanding of Steiner's lectures that "Steiner created an archetype for all future true karma research : the karma researcher as such, is entitled to reveal the karma of others only once he has revealed his own, but *it is at his own discretion whether he does so directly, or indirectly.* That Steiner did not do so directly is understandable, particularly with reference to a classic rule in all mystery wisdom : the initiate must keep silent about himself."

A paragraph later is introduced with the following words : "I am fully aware that in doing this [publishing my own karmic antecedents - Ed] I am breaching the previously totally necessary occult modesty which was the characteristic of all of Steiner's work". Saether claims to find the grounds for his own occult immodesty in Steiner's lectures yet it has proved impossible for these readers to find any logical thread in his argument: Saether tries to justify his own point of view by using Steiner as grounds for breaching a key principle in Steiner's work.

Sæther's claim that "the karma researcher is only entitled to reveal the karma of others once he has revealed his own" is not an idea that we can find can find in Steiner's own work.

"Radical Intimacy" - For Whom?

Saether is perfectly free in our opinion to (as he puts it) "...have chosen to stand out as a point of reference for others who are in search of something or doing research", but we feel that his attempt to contribute something new to anthroposophical karma research lacks certain essential qualities. It is simply not sufficient that one claims at the outset to have followed indications by Rudolf Steiner and writes "my method, which is the one given by Rudolf Steiner..." when the clarity, modesty and moral responsibility which have to be present in such an undertaking not only are lacking to the extent they are here, but are set aside by Saether's own method. This becomes quite explicit in our opinion when he speaks of what he calls "radical intimacy". He writes for instance: "During intimate conversations I have revealed intimate relationships to and about anthroposophists, also about other contemporaries without the latter being informed of this, when *I have judged* the situation to be right for such radical intimacy..." How Saether should be in a position to judge to what extent participants in courses, lectures etc. have done the necessary preparation and arrived at the balance and maturity which are necessary for work in this area, we cannot begin to understand, and we can find nothing in what he writes which gives us confidence that he possesses such powers of judgement. This "radical intimacy" seems to be a device which is supposed to permit Saether to approach other people with what could be emotionally charged ideas about their own karmic background. He does not set out his criteria for such a *judgement* and he cannot know in advance what its consequences might be, quite apart from the fact that people have no means of protecting themselves from these consequences and that he is placing himself in a certain position of power over others. One is reminded of the late 1960's when certain hippies saw it as their task to "turn people on" in their surroundings without the latter having asked for this assistance. This was done by putting LSD in their food or drink without them knowing. We have encountered similar phenomena in our practices where people have had to struggle for years with the consequences of various "therapies" or self-development .

Saether postulates his own rights without seeming to be clear about or bothering about his own responsibility or about the consequences of his actions for the people around him. When working with patients, whether in psychiatry or in general practice, it is an ideal to provide the conditions within which people can make independent decisions and as far as possible deal with life on their own terms. This is necessary not only out of basic respect for a fellow human being but also because we know that change and development which are based on one's own understanding and own choices are in the long term more fruitful to the individual concerned. Saether claims that he is entitled to decide what a fellow human being should be confronted with. In doing so he is apparently also giving himself the right to take a position of power vis-à-vis the person he is exposing to "radical intimacy". He appears to ignore the fact that intimacy involves the ability and the desire for closeness in both parties to a relationship and this concept of his seems to lack both the mutuality and the closeness. In certain situations such an inflicted intimacy could more easily be seen as a violation. This should be elementary knowledge for anyone working with human development. Saether however sees no problem in assessing his right to practise "radical intimacy". In a scientific context, within which Saether clearly feels his work belongs, one would have to analyse such a concept before one could use it as the basis for any kind of practice. When on top of this he departs radically from the core of what he himself claims as his starting point, namely anthroposophical knowledge, this "radical intimacy" is exposed as a personal "product". The scientific basis for both the concept and its social application is lacking. Thus from our point of view Saether's articles turn out to be testimonies to his own activities and intentions but ones in which questions of scientific method and other people's development and freedom are of secondary importance.

Karma Research Is Dangerous - But For Whom?

Towards the end of the article Saether attempts to justify his research within the context of anthroposophical endeavour. He writes: "the question needs to be asked to what extent a free cultural life exists at all in Norway or indeed in other countries and it is linked with the question of whether the School of Spiritual Science can make room for spiritual researchers other than Rudolf Steiner and if so whether it is entitled to create the conditions for such research." These may be very interesting questions to raise in certain circumstances, but we can see nothing in Saether's work that is relevant to them. A little later he goes on to say: "As we know, after Rudolf Steiner's death karma research came to be seen not only as presumptious and impossible but also as dangerous to society. Opinions such as these were and still are in my view the expression of an occult attack on anthroposophy itself and thus also on Rudolf Steiner. The time has now come to put this right." We too are convinced that the foundations and justification for the existence of the Anthroposophical Society is a creative activity which includes the areas Saether is concerned with. However our comment on these allegations is that they are erroneous and historically unsound. He ignores the fact that many individuals and groups have concerned themselves with "his" topic over a long period of time and have also done so in specific professional contexts. The majority have followed Rudolf Steiner's advice and have themselves felt an obvious moral obligation to handle this with modesty and discretion and not to speak of any experiences they may have had in this area other than to those closest to them. It is in the nature of this work that the results appear primarily in the conduct of the individual's life and in the individual's morality in a variety of life situations. Saether seems to believe that reticence in this area is linked with a so-called "occult attack" on anthroposophy and Rudolf Steiner. This view is more than a little remarkable given that Steiner himself emphasised reticence and modesty in the way that we have referred to above and given that these qualities are among the pre-conditions he mentioned in everything to do with this subject. Other methods which lack these qualities may on the other hand very well involve danger, both to others and to the individual concerned.

Saether's "Imaginations"

To conclude we should like to make a few comments on Saether's concept of imaginations as he describes them in "A meditative life in relation to destiny questions". In this article he writes: " Then with a "wrench" I was led back to around 400 BC into a situation in a former life in Greece. I saw myself and also recognised another person from today in that former incarnation [.....]. My awareness of the time and the place were so abundantly clear that I could immediately find my bearings."

We have no doubt that Saether has had inner experiences but we do have questions about the nature of these experiences. Rudolf Steiner emphasises that assessing the reality of an imagination is of critical importance and that this process is governed by its own rules.

We are struck by the fact that Rudolf Steiner does not use the expression "imagination" when he speaks of the karma exercise, but rather: "an image which is raised into the spirit from out of the physical body" (Dornach, 9.5.24). He introduces his discussion of the exercise with the words: "It is possible to attain a relatively quick maturing of one's understanding of karmic connections if over a long period of time one patiently and energetically tries to allow those things to play into one's consciousness which otherwise would also be present there but are not properly grasped and are lost in the concerns of everyday life."

This transformation out of the physical body could be deemed to explain why the images Saether describes have such strongly physical characteristics, but there are other possible interpretations. The "clear outlines" might also indicate that the images have elements of projection from daytime consciousness and memories even though Saether does point out the difference between imaginations and memories. This interpretation is supported by the fact that Saether's method involves moving backwards in his biography through the power of suggestion and out of the physical environment, rather than limiting itself to the concrete experiences of daily life which are the starting point for the karma exercise. This considerably enhances the possibility of errors and inaccuracies among other reasons because physical processes can be raised into consciousness and express themselves in the form of images or as impressions comparable with outer sense impressions.

Imaginative experiences arising from work with exercises may well have the characteristics of our physical surroundings to a greater or lesser extent but after a while these experiences will take on a different quality, free from physical experiences and having a greater inherent reality. Saether mentions that as one progresses with this work one "gets to know" beings in the world of the elementals, friends who have crossed the threshold of death, the so-called double and other spiritual beings. Both in his books and in the School of Spiritual Science, Rudolf Steiner described the encounter with the "guardian of the threshold" and with the forces of the double as central to all meditative work in our age. Development that takes place without constant reference to the "guardian of the threshold" and without the difficult experience of, and working on, the being of the double lacks essential qualities. We find this aspect lacking, both in Saether's articles and in the lectures he has given in Oslo. We therefore wonder where his path of experience stands in relation to this essential encounter with the guardian and the consequent repeated confrontation with one's own moral qualities.

In addition to querying the justification for calling Saether's images "imaginations" in Rudolf Steiner's sense of the word, we also wonder on what basis Saether is able to feel so sure about the reality of what he describes. In a lecture to teachers Steiner says the following: "The next stage in meditation { after imagination, Ed.} involves acquiring the ability to allow these images to disappear completely again. There is something fascinating about them and if the human being does not develop them in complete freedom, as one would in a meditation, they can fasten on him like parasites." (Dornach 26.12.21, GA 303). Later on Steiner describes how if one can consciously extinguish these imaginative pictures, something can come through from behind the veil of the senses. By disappearing out of one's consciousness, they allow something that is resounding inwardly to manifest. Only by means of such a process does it become possible to form a judgement on the content of the imaginative experiences.

Saether says that the imaginations "may contain elements of the consciousness that belongs to imagination and intuition". In *Occult Science* Rudolf Steiner writes : "...for anyone who is wishing to understand the human being by means of imagination and inspiration alone the processes which go on in the innermost part of the human being will elude their consciousness. Thus it is only intuitive knowledge which permits research into repeated lives on earth and karma. Anything which purports to be the truth about these processes must stem from research by means of intuitive faculties. If the human being wishes to gain knowledge of himself and his own being, he can only do so through intuition. Intuition enables one to perceive what it is that passes from one life on earth to another."

It must be entirely up to each individual to freely choose impulses and ideas as nourishment for his own development and understanding. The consciousness that belongs to our age faces a strong challenge in this. Our consciousness must find a path in the tension between fantastic mysticism on the one hand and the fiction of closed systems of reference on the other. Anthroposophical knowledge can be seen to be connected to a third way. On this path it is more important to ask who I am than who I was.

So who am I?

This will become apparent in the biography which I modestly weave into the web of humanity's further destiny.

Published in abridged translation by kind permission of ANTHROPOSOFISK SELSKAP, NORGE, Meddelelser til medlemmene.

Book Review

Because of Yolande

by Dorit Winter

Golden Gate Publications, Mountain View, California 1997

This little book, which would challenge the wit of anyone trying to assign it to a particular genre, takes on the one level the form of a meditative diary of an author reflecting upon her own life; on another level it is the chronicle of the life of an imaginary (but in another sense very real) Jewish victim of the Nazi holocaust; and on a third level - which represents the fusion of the first two - it explores the relationship between individual destiny and the destiny of mankind as a whole, guided as it is by the Cosmic Christ and His servant, or countenance, Michael. In so far as there can be said to be a main theme, recurring like a familiar melody through all the rich medley of ideas and interludes, it is the investigation of the extent to which every earthly act or happening is but the reflection of a hidden web of destiny. More specifically, it focuses on the devastating effect upon souls incarnating since the Second World War of what was brought into the spiritual world especially by those who suffered and died in the Nazi concentration camps. For

> "it was their trauma, but it is our syndrome. And the symptoms affect not just the established group known as Children of Survivors. It affects also the apparently unconnected,... whose condition amounts to an inability to properly incarnate. They are not retarded; they are ill. And the origins of their illness cannot be found by any

> doctor. For the origins of their illnesses are not physical. They are the soul-spiritual disorders induced by pre-earthly trauma: the pain and torment and aborted life forces of fifty million dead."

Plainly put, the book is about the Nazi holocaust and its continuing relevance for our time.

However, such a description does not even remotely do *Because of Yolande* justice. In a very real sense, the book is not about anything: rather is it an invitation by the author to set out with her on a journey of discovery. A reader who does not want to set forth but prefers to be instructed or entertained may find the manner of writing somewhat infuriating, flitting as the book does between different themes, different levels of reality. Such a reader may also feel irritated that he is constantly being invited to join in the creative process of the book's writing. However, this is not a book for consumption, rather does it invite participation. And that participation is a process of self-discovery. It is a book that one cannot properly read without becoming to some extent a different person.

Who will want to read such a book? Although it does not require any prior knowledge of anthroposophy and is free from jargon and hackneyed phrases, it is not written for a mass market. Clearly, the publishing world had no enthusiasm for bringing it into the light of day. That it has appeared at all is due to the commitment of a small group of the author's students at the Rudolf Steiner College in San Francisco. This raises a crucial question: how are literary works of this nature, deeply imbued as they are by a sincere, unapologetic commitment to spiritual science, to reach those needing to read them? One might have thought that this was the job of the anthroposophical presses. But this will not happen for as long as these presses have to vie for their position in the global market-place. One way or another - and whether this happens through subsidising the existing presses or through publishing initiatives such as the one which brought out *Because of Yolande* probably does not make all that much difference, except in the cost - we need increasingly to engage in the kind of "samizdat" (self-publishing) activity which kept true culture alive in Soviet Russia. For what is the significance of publishing in our time? What do we seek to communicate in the age of the consciousness soul? The mass publishing market is dominated by the wish to impart information (or sell entertainment), for "information is power". But this is largely irrelevant in an age which should be reaching out beyond the intellectual soul, where the individual human I is still seeking to raise itself to maturity and tries to dominate the world around it. The author of *Because of Yolande* is courageously communicating <u>herself</u> and is as such making a worthy offering to any who may be wanting to develop this self which has been wrested at such cost from obscurity by that Being who is the ultimate subject of the book:

> "This is a story about someone writing a story about someone",

as Dorit Winter states in her first sentence.

All who are interested in pursuing such a path of development are urged to read this book, preferably more than once.

Simon Blaxland-de Lange

Notes on the Contributors

Dorit Winter is Founder and Director of the San Francisco Waldorf Teacher Training of Rudolf Steiner College. Her most recent book is *Sheets of White Light*, a collection of seven short stories, Rudolf Steiner College Press, 1999.

Henning Köhler works in curative education and for many years worked at the Filderklinik. He has specialised in psychosomatic disorders in adolescence, behavioural disorders in children and anorexia.

Doré Deverell has toured and lectured extensively on the theme of her successful publication *Light Beyond The Darkness,* Temple Lodge, 1996.

Mathias Wais works in a counselling centre for parents and children in Dortmund specialising in biography work and in counselling for abusers and the abused.

Coralee Schmandt is a eurythmist with an academic background in American and English literature. She is currently one of the carriers of the Orientation Programme at Emerson College.

Nick Thomas's most recent publication is *Science between Space and Counterspace* which contains the results of his extensive research into the Science of the Spirit as illuminated by the methods of modern projective geometry.

Bob Dudney has been a family doctor for twenty years in California and is also a faculty member of the San Francisco Waldorf Teaching Program.

Smit, Enge and *Schage* are all anthroposophical doctors working in Norway.

Back numbers 45 - 48 (49 has been sold out) are available from Floris Books 15 Harrison Gardens Edinburgh EH11 1SH £6.99 each

Back numbers 41 - 44, 50 and 51 are available from The Editors Emerson College Forest Row East Sussex RH18 5JX £3 each - £5 for two Numbers 50 and 51 £7

51
TOGETHER ON EARTH

We are part of many different communities, the ones we are born into, the ones we live in, the ones we work in, the ones we consciously join and build together. How do these varying configurations of more or less consciously chosen destiny companions enable us to realise our individual and social potential ? We find ourselves in manifold human constellations on this planet, in specific geographical locations, and with particular connections to the earth itself. In some ways we have come to experience this as one world rich in human diversity, in other ways the divisions on the globe seem to mock any notion of our being together on earth. How do the conditions in which we live together on earth make it possible for us to fulfil our individual and shared destinies ? How does our relationship to the earth itself affect these tasks ? How awake are we in our consciousness on earth to the spiritual communities that we are also part of ?

The Golden Blade 50
1998

WORKING WITH DESTINY II
The Practice of Karma Research

A Fiftieth Birthday Salute
Owen Barfield

Karma Experience, Research and the Power of Empathy
Baruch Urieli

Anthroposophical Medical Work and Karma Consciousness
Maurice Orange

Biography Work: Awakening to Destiny
Margli Matthews

Research Techniques and Life Events
Jostein Saether

Discerning Destiny
Harlan Gilbert

Shakespeare and World Destiny
Richard Ramsbotham

Reincarnation Therapy
Trui Derwig

Karma and Altered States of Consciousness
Willem Veltman

The Uses of Adversity
Christopher Clouder

Touchstone
Elizabeth Attwell

The Golden Blade 44
1992

EUROPE AND THE WEST

The Spiritual Contribution of the West
Virginia Sease

Language and Nationhood
William Forward

Are we detached ?
Andrew Wolpert

An Interfering Interest
Peter Tradowsky

Breathing and Circulation
Jenny Josephson

First Aid at the Turn of the Century
Jenny Josephson

Prometheus Unbound
Andrew Welburn

The Golden Blade 43
1991

EUROPE

Central Europe between East and West
Rudolf Steiner

The Spiritual Tasks of Central Europe
Sergei. O. Prokofieff

The Heart and Lungs
Jenny Josephson

The Emergence of Europe
Coenraad van Houten

For the Conscience of Europe
Charles Lawrie

The Soul and Spirit of a People
Athys Floride

Present Tasks of Central Europe
Manfred Schmidt - Brabant

In Memoriam for Adam Bittleston

The Golden Blade 42
1990

FREEDOM AND DESTINY

Man, Offspring of the World of Stars
Rudolf Steiner

The Observation of the Stars
John Meeks & Michael Brinch

The Life between Death and Rebirth
Elizabeth Vreede

The Bridge of the Green Snake
A. Bockemül

Rainer Maria Rilke
Rudi Lissau

Deeds in the Life of William Mann
Roswitha Spence

William Mann - The Teacher
Ted Roberts

Addiction as an Impulse towards Renewal
J. van der Haar

The Destiny of the American Indian
Brian Gold

The Golden Blade 41
1989

THE EARTH AS A SEED

What is the Earth in reality
Rudolf Steiner

David Newbatt- An Artist in Midstream
Carola Kindle

Three Great Ideals in our Time
Rudolf Steiner

The Light of the World
Owen Barfield

Technology and the Earth
Nick Thomas

Puppets Help in a Mixed-up World
Gisela Bittleston

Man and Nature in Different Cultures
Andreas Suchantke

The Many Faces of Water
Mark Riegner

The Powers of Sorrow
Georg Kühlewind

The Golden Blade 48
1996

THE IMAGE OF BLOOD

The Mystery of Blood
James Dyson

The Bleeding Wound of King Amfortas
Karal Jan Tusenius

D.H. Lawrence's The Rainbow, The Lion, and the Blood of Sophia
Andrew Welburn

Mithras, The Bull, and the Transformation of the Blood
Christopher Clouder

Of Blood and Money
Christopher Houghton Budd

Money - The Christ Blood of The Threefold Social Order
Jack Foster

Chosen Destiny
Rudi Lissau

The Golden Blade 47
1995

THE QUEST FOR THE GRAIL

The Matter of Britain
Richard Seddon

The Polarity of Parzival and Gawain
Frank Teichmann

The Emergence of the Grail Legend
Hanah May Thomas

The Temple of the Grail
John Meeks

Eschenbach and Michelangelo
Andrew Wolpert

"Redemption for the Redeemer"
Alex Naylor

The Play of the Planets in Eschenbach's *Parzival*
William Forward

The Quest in New York City in 1994
Barbara Francis

The Golden Blade 46
1994

CHAOS, RHYTHM AND FLOW IN NATURE

The Universe as Organism
Lawrence Edwards

Chaos Theory and Projective Geometry
Nick Thomas

Our Heart: Sounding, Serving, Unifying
Philip Kilner

Learning to Enhance Sense-perception
Olive Whicher

Flow Design Research
John Wilkes

The Golden Blade 45
1993

CHANGE IN A CHANGING WORLD

Celebrating Columbus
Paul Law

Upheaval in Adolescence
William Forward

Centring the Teacher
Dorit Winter

Mystery Play is Now
Christopher Marcus

Regenerative Grammar
Andrew Wolpert

Losing Ground
Ria Freiermuth

Finding One's Place
Stephen Briault

The Flowering of the Soul in Florence
Charles Lawrie